Spring Publications, Inc.
P.O. Box 222069
Dallas, Texas 75222

SOUL AND MONEY

Russell A. Lockhart
James Hillman
Arwind Vasavada
John Weir Perry
Joel Covitz
Adolf Guggenbühl-Craig

1982

ACKNOWLEDGMENTS

The six articles composing this volume were originally presented as speeches at an International Congress of Jungian Analysts.

Kate Smith Passy designed the cover; Mary Helen Gray supervised production. Maribeth Lipscomb and Gerald Burns lent assistance; Cheryl Rasmussen Kohler typeset the book.

Printed in the United States of America by Sheegog Printing Co., Dallas, Texas.

Library of Congress Cataloging in Publication Data
Main entry under title:
Soul and money.

   Proceedings of the 8th international congress of the International Association for Analytical Psychology, held in August 1980, San Francisco.
   Contents: Coins and psychological change / Russell A. Lockhart — A contribution to soul and money / James Hillman — Fee-less practice and soul work / Arwind Vasavada — [etc.]
   1. Money—Psychological aspects—Congresses. 2. Psychoanalysis—Congresses.
   I. Lockhart, Russell A., 1938—   . II. International Association for Analytical Psychology.
HG222.3.S65   332.4'01'9   81-84495
ISBN 0-88214-318-2   AACR2

C O N T E N T S

Coins and Psychological Change

By Russell A. Lockhart

When I was a child I would frequently disappear into the closet of my bedroom. After locking the door I turned on a flashlight covered with blue plastic and began to dismantle what my mother called a "pile of junk." It was old toys, books, papers, clothes. What my mother didn't know—what no one in the whole world knew—was that this pile of junk was an elaborate camouflage serving as a hiding place for a secret. My secret was an old kitchen matchbox filled with silver coins—nickels, dimes, quarters. I would unearth these coins and in that strange blue light I would begin imagining. I imagined great riches and abundant wealth. I knew the meaning of a Plutonic affair! But more than riches, gazing into the silvery objects excited my imagination generally. The coins had a strong generative effect. It is said that money begets money. But then I knew that money begets imaginal worlds. I knew too that begetting had something to do with sex. I had not yet been aware of the curious relation between spending sexually, spending energy, spending time and spending money. Or yet with problems of saving oneself sexually, saving time, saving energy, saving money. Then, I was spending time with coins I would never spend. These imaginal adventures stimulated by my coins were my most valued experiences. Occasionally, I would be awakened out of my reveries by my mother pounding on the door wanting to know what I was doing. Tact prohibits going into this further than to say that my first experiences with synchronicity were in those moments of correspondence between my mother's suspicions and the full extent of my imaginal explorations.

One afternoon I came home from school and with my usual enthusiasm went for my closet and my secret coins. I was shocked by what I found. The closet floor was bare, cleaned out, swept clean. I looked frantically for my coins. I could not find them. My secret coins were gone. I ran out to the trash but the cans were empty. My coins were such a secret I could not bring myself to ask about them. I never went back to my closet again to spend those hours imagining. Something was broken in me with this loss. Shortly afterwards, I developed a severe case of measles that turned into mastoiditis and I was hospitalized. Even then, I connected the loss of my secret coins with my illness. The effect of this experience was that I wanted to become a doctor. I forgot about my coins. I forgot about imagining. I turned my attention to the world and dropped childish things. From that time until I was in graduate school I had no dreams. My coins, my imagination, even my dreams were gone.

Some months ago this dream came to me:

> I was sitting at my typewriter. Suddenly, the typewriter stopped working. I opened the cover and found a matchbox in the mechanism. I opened the matchbox and it was full of coins. I put it aside, closed the cover, and went on typing.

A short while after this dream, Dr. James Hillman called and presented me with an invitation to speak at the International Congress of Analytical Psychology on the subject of money. Why he did this I do not know. I can assure you that I have no special knowledge or wisdom about money. To be speaking on money strikes me as an enormous inflation. But I accepted the challenge in part as a way of honoring the return of my childhood coins.

I was excited about the return of my coins. It seemed so right to be writing on money under the auspices of an image that in childhood had so connected me to imagination and soul and body. But something was wrong. Try as I might I could not write. Months went by. My typewriter was stopped. Of course! The dream had shown that the coins stopped my typewriter. In my excitement over the coins I had neglected to see this. In the dream it was when I put the coins aside that I could go on typing. But how could I write on money and put aside my coins? In the dream I could do that but in the reality of the everyday world I could not. The call of my coins was too strong.

What follows then is not a scholarly piece on the psychology of money. Nor have I attempted a Jungian approach to the meaning of money in analytical practice or in everyday life in any formal or theoretically suitable way. All these things are, of course, vital issues to us, worthy of pursuit. But here, in these few pages, I have to follow the lead of my coins, letting them be psychopomp once again.

In the spring I went to Scotland. I had labored for months on money and had come to nothing. A trainee seemed to say more in a humorous remark than I had with all my effort. He said: ''Money is like sex: there's never enough of either.'' But surely in Scotland I would find something on money that would release me from the quagmire in which I found myself. I decided to collect some stories from the old tradition-bearers in the Western Highlands. I received many stories but none about money, although I heard one proverb that excited something in my own Scottish blood. As a Jungian analyst I have tended often to focus on the roundness of coins, their inherent mandalic quality, their relation to energy and to values, and their imaging of the Self. This Scottish proverb was a jolt to my lazy thinking. ''Money,'' say the Scotch, ''is flat and is meant to be piled up.'' So typically Scottish to notice the forgotten characteristic and to remember the utility of things!

In the middle of a dark storm I found my way to Dunvegan Castle, ancestral home of the Clan McCloud on the Island of Skye. I fell into a long talk with a castle guide who was full of stories and delighted to have a willing ear. As we stood under the famous Fairy Flag, I asked him for a story about money. He thought for a while, looked downcast, and said he didn't know any. Then, with a twinkle as elfish as I have ever seen, he said he had one that might do. It seemed that one day a farmer's cow had wandered too near one of the high cliffs and, tripping on some small boulders, had fallen over the edge. Down below, in the loch, a fisherman was lazily fishing in his drifting boat. Well, the cow landed in the boat, destroying it completely, and managing to kill herself in the bargain. The two men got into a terrible row over who was at fault. The owner of the cow claimed that if the fisherman had not been so carelessly adrift the cow would have fallen harmlessly in the water. The owner of the boat claimed that had the herdsman not been so careless in letting his cow near the edge, she would not have fallen. Unable to settle their dispute, they took the matter to the Chief. The Chief was thrown into an enormous conflict and just couldn't decide what was just. So he called in his wiseman—what we would now obviously call his analyst—and asked his advice. ''Chief,'' the analyst said, ''you must pay both men, for it was the rock on your ground that would not hold and the waves in your loch that brought the boat where it lay.''

I was struck immediately by how extraordinarily difficult it is in money matters, which seem so heavily characterized by the either/or-ness of gain and loss, have and have not, spend and save, how difficult to find the wisdom of that third position.

On this trip I discovered something in my ancestral background that seemed curiously connected with both my interests in healing and my renewed interest in coins. In 1329, a band of Scottish knights set out on a crusade to the Holy Land. Their leader, Lord Douglas, carried about his neck a silver box containing the heart of Robert the Bruce who had labored to free Scotland from English rule but who had died before making a pilgrimage to the Holy Land. Alongside Douglas rode Sir Symon Locard who had been knighted by Bruce, and was now entrusted with the task of carrying and safeguarding the key to the heart box. Eventually, they rode into battle against the Saracens in Spain. Douglas was killed but Sir Symon Locard's gallantry saved the heart box. Afterwards, to commemorate the event, Locard's name was changed to "Lockheart," and shortened finally to "Lockhart." A heart within a fetterlock became the family coat of arms with the motto *"corda serata pando,"* meaning "I open locked hearts."

During this battle, Symon captured an Emir prince of wealth and distinction. In paying a heavy ransom of gold and silver, the prince's mother dropped a jewel from her bag. My wily ancestor demanded that it be included in the ransom. Of course the mother acquiesced rather than lose her son and told Sir Symon that it was an ancient healing stone, a sovereign and holy remedy against all manner of ills. During the reign of Edward the Fourth, the jewel, a deep red triangular stone, was mounted on a silver coin, and since that time has been known as the Lee Penny after the ancestral home of the Lockharts in the Lee and Carnwath area of Southern Scotland. The Lee Penny is now held by Simon Macdonald Lockhart, current holder of the lands of Lee, who graciously hosted me during my recent visit and gave me the chance to be alone with the jewel.

In holding the Lee Penny and admiring the gold box made to hold it, which was presented to the Lockhart family by Maria Teresa, the Empress Queen of Austria, I was strangely excited and began to experience a flood of flashing images of things I had never experienced before. The stone was alive. This talisman, which served as the impetus to Sir Walter Scott's novel, *The Talisman*, has a remarkable history of healing and an intriguing manner of exerting its power. The ritual for evoking its talismanic power is to dip it into water with "two dips and a swirl." During this rite words must not be spoken. Speaking renders the stone ineffectual. This aspect of the rite had a very curious effect on me, on one whose work is so related to the word. Water so treated can be used to heal wounds, diseases of cattle, and all manner of things, and there are many recorded instances of such effects. I can attest to the power inherent in this talisman but am reminded, too, of my host's words in his book on the history of the Lockhart family: "Pride in the possession of a charm filched from a desperate mother is not the most glorious of qualities."[1]

But the talismanic nature of the Lee Penny has haunted me ever since I held it in my hands. My attempts to write on money were bogged down, and my intense preoccupation with the talisman as a healing charm kept interfering. The image of activating its power by saying nothing kept swirling about my psyche and nearly rendered me mute. Then, quite by accident, my attention was called to Chapter 99 of Herman Melville's *Moby Dick.*

II

Riveted to the mainmast of the *Pequod* was a gold coin, a large Ecuadorian doubloon, the prize for raising the great white whale. It was, as Melville tells it, the talisman of Moby Dick. The image gripped me. Compelling also was a curious picture, the gold coin and the Lee Penny etching themselves together. I knew the gold coin was an image of the Self as was Moby Dick. But assimilating images to a concept of the Self was not very engaging. I find little life in this. But I frequently find life in the connection between images, in the manner in which they are linked, in what I call the "eros bond" between images. In Melville's story, the images of coin and whale are linked through the image of *talisman*. It was this link that began to dance in my mind together with the talisman of the Lockhart clan.

I found in Dr. Edinger's masterful commentary on *Moby Dick* an exciting and confirming observation. He said of this link that it was "an organic connection between the symbolic meaning of the coin and that of the whale."[2] To me, Edinger's use of the word "organic" was crucial, because it pointed to the living quality of the link between coin and whale. The idea that the coin and whale were symbols of the Self was dry to me because I knew it already. But the image of the coin as a talisman of the Self was one I did not know, and it felt full of life and portent.

Melville must have known of the living and organic capacity of the Self to ensoul the objects of our experience and their relationships in the psyche. In writing on the coin he gave this ensoulment a peculiar and intriguing cast when he said: "And some certain significance lurks in all things, else all things are of little worth, and the round world itself but an empty cipher."[3] In Melville's imagination, the very world is ensouled with value and worth, a significance that "lurks" in all things. It was this image of *lurking* that captured for me the living organic quality. To say that meaning "lurks" in all things leads at once to that metaphorical interiority where one can hear that meaning "lies in wait," that meaning is "ready to ambush," that meaning moves about "furtively," "sneakily," "secretly," that meaning lives and breathes unobserved, unsuspected, concealed, hidden from view. In such an imaginal underworld, meaning itself becomes personified, a living one, living in the dark, in the shadows, obscured, watching, waiting, looking for the right moment to work its will. It is true that we may find meaning. It is also true that meaning finds us.

I realized, of course, that the gold coin, in addition to being a symbol of the Self and a talisman of Moby Dick was, in fact, *money.* Perhaps nothing else (lest it be sexuality) seemed to me so hard, so real, so concrete, so literal, yet so quickly symbolized, interpreted, or translated into something else. As I puzzled on this I realized that one aspect of this lies in the nature of money itself: *money is the most powerful, practical and experienced form of transformation.* In the most starkly real way, one can turn money into anything in the world. Nothing else achieves this range of transformational possibility in actuality or in fantasy. In this direct sense, money symbolizes everything. Byron went correctly to the heart of the matter when he observed that "every guinea is a philosopher's stone."[4] The life and soul of money must lie in this transformational potentiality. This is also the deepest reason for the psyche to be drawn into a fascination with money. As with the search for alchemical gold, or the search for true love, one experiences something of the possibility of transformation in oneself when in the grips of the transformational power of money. I suppose that's why, when one is in the depths of a leaden depression, spending money will lift the spirit.

Reflecting on the gold coin as money and Moby Dick as a personification of the Self produced a most curious statement that would not leave me alone: *money is a talisman of the Self.* What could this mean? A talisman is an object invested with 'supernatural' power that can be effectively and actively called upon to exert its effects to achieve certain ends. It is to be distinguished from ''amulet'' in that an amulet passively wards off evil by deflection. Clearly, a talisman carries an active transformative power. The talismanic power of money lies in its transformational nature. Since talismanic power can be invested in any object, it follows that any object can become money.

If money is a talisman of the Self, then the Self must use money to achieve its aims. Such a strange statement is in contrast to the more usual emphasis on the ego's use and relation to money. Yet, there is a talismanic power that lurks in money, and that power is invested there by the Self. When we confront the power of money in our lives, we are confronting the power of the 'other' in us, a power that works its will in and through money. It is the Self. It was this power I experienced long ago with my coins in the closet. The Self used the coins to transform my everyday world into a world of psyche.

At this point I could have gone into the history and significance of talismans and amplified all manner of interesting and powerful images concerning talismans and their use and how all of this could be seen in our behavior and relationships to money. Perhaps another time. Instead, I was gripped once again by what Paul Valery had noticed:

> You have certainly observed the curious fact that a given *word* which is perfectly clear when you hear it or use it in *everyday* language, and which does not give rise to any difficulty when it is engaged in the rapid movement of an ordinary sentence becomes magically embarrassing, introduces a strange resistance, frustrates any effort at definition as soon as you take it out of circulation to examine it separately and look for its meaning after taking away its instantaneous function . . . . we understand ourselves thanks only to *the speed of our passages past words* . . . .[5]

And once again I was gripped by my own fascination with words.

Had I not myself written:

> Current meaning and definition are too often only the shell of a word. We use words but do not know their soul—or even care. We are all word abusers. Anything that will help free us from the prison of current meaning, the literalness and speed of the present, will help us to free Psyche from her prison shell. Words take on life, induce images, excite the imagination, begin to weave textures with one another and tell whole stories if we but scratch the surface of the word.[6]

So, if I was to follow this idea of "money as talisman of the Self," I would have to follow the words. Words, like coins, are realms where meaning lurks.

I approached this statement by taking each one of the central word images out of circulation: *money, talisman, Self.* One way I do this is by going into a kind of "etymological reverie" in an attempt to uncover and release the old word meanings that are still alive but forgotten. The unconscious remembers these old meanings, remembers the entire history of a word's story. But the conscious mind needs to be reminded.

I began with "talisman." It is a French and Spanish noun, masculine as befits its character of active power. It was imported from the Arabic *tilsaman*, a plural of *tilsam.* This in turn was a loan word from the Greek *telesma. Telesma* referred to "a ceremony of consecration" and was a name for the "mysteries." It was derived from an earlier Greek word, *telein,* which meant "to fulfill," "to initiate into the mysteries," and "to pay." Variations of these words referred to money paid to fulfill obligations and debts, money paid to enter the priesthood, and money paid as part of the mystery rites. It is clear from the history of the word "talisman" that initiation into mysteries, completion and fulfillment, and payment in money belong together.

Questions began to stir. How does the Self use money to render something sacred? How can money consecrate the work we do in analysis? Is the money paid by a patient payment for initiation into the mysteries of the Self? I remembered Tertullian's admonition that "nothing that is God's is obtainable by money," and Thoreau's echo: "money is not required to buy one necessity of the soul." But are we not workers of the soul? Do we not engage the necessities of the soul in our work? If so, money *is* required to buy connection to soul, connection to psyche, and connection to Self through us. The roots of talisman tell me that the sacred mysteries and money belong together.

The word *telein* comes from the Greek word *telos*. This meant "fulfillment" and "completeness" in the sense of reaching an end, a purpose, a final goal. Going back further, into the prehistory of the language, the reconstructed Indo-European root for *telos* is $*q^{w}el$. This root contains the basic image of "revolving," "moving around a fixed point," "dwelling within." The same root gave rise to the Latin *colere* meaning "to cultivate" which became our English word "culture"; the Old English *hweol* which became the English "wheel"; and the Greek *kiklos* meaning "wheel."

To experience the talismanic nature of something is to experience being turned, being revolved, being pulled to dwell within, encircled. It is an early experience that led to the words of circles, cycles, wheels. A talisman works not in linear ways but by turning, moving around, circulating. This turning, as telos, has to do with one's fate, one's purpose, one's end. Turning points are talismanic moments when we are turned toward our fate. Money as talisman of the Self now tells us that the Self works through money toward our telos, our purpose, our end. Our relation to money must carry evidence of our telos. Money functions as talisman when it turns us, forces us, moves us into confrontation with our telos. Our telos, our final end, our purpose is said to determine our worth. When we are asked, "What are you worth?" do not the money images come bound with all other considerations? In this sense it is not surprising that the word "worth" comes from an Indo-European root which means "to turn" and "to bend" and which yields up such words as the Old English *wyrd* meaning "fate" and "destiny" and which became our English word "weird." Here also is the Old English *writhan*, meaning "to twist" and "to torture," becoming our word "writhe." Nested here is the Old English *wyrgan* meaning "to strangle," which became the English "worry." Embedded here is the Greek word *rhombus* meaning "magic wheel" and the Old English *wyrm* meaning "worm," as well as the Latin *vermis* meaning "vermin."

Thus, the worth of someone is deeply tied to images of destiny, the twists and turns of fate, and the wheels of fortune. The same is true of money. Our relation to money is our relation to fate. Our relation to money is our relation to purpose, end, goal, telos. Money as talisman emphasizes this, and money as talisman of the Self emphasizes the ways and means through the twists and turns and circulation of money that the Self brings us, turns us round, toward our telos. Ego, it seems to me, always has a straight purpose, the goal laid out in plain sight, the end always in view. Ego eyes are always on the tangent straight ahead. But the Self works to turn us from such straightness, and it uses money to do so. It turns us around a deeper axis, and we cannot see with open eyes where this turning takes us. A deeper kind of 'seeing' is required—the seeing of the mysteries. The basic meaning of the word "mystery" is "seeing with the eyes closed."

Does any of this echo in the word "money" itself? The modern English word "money" is from the Middle English *monoie* which comes from the Old French feminine noun *monie*. This in turn was a development from the Latin word *moneta*—also a feminine noun. Although this is not the place to carry on about the significance of word gender, it is striking that the word for money, so often considered a masculine province, is itself feminine. There is something even more deeply feminine about the word. It is the Latin name for the mother of the Muses who in Greek was called *Mnemosyne*. She was the goddess of memory. Thus out of the matrix or womb of memory come those creative engenderers we call the Muses who go into the name for minting, coining, and money. Money hides within its name the creative muses and their source in memory.

There is more. We find next that *Moneta* was an epithet, a name, for Juno, Queen Mother of Heaven. It was, in fact, in Juno's temple where the money was minted. This came about in the following way. A Roman army was losing a battle and was nearly out of money. This caused dissension, demoralization and loss of spirit. In a desperate attempt to find an answer to their plight they consulted Juno. She advised them that if their cause was just and they fought for their cause the money would be forthcoming. The soldiers rallied around this image and fought on. Soon, money arrived from Rome and the battle was won. As a tribute to Juno's wise counsel, the mint was set up in her temple which housed as well the Roman treasury. All of this puts money matters, we might say as well the *matter* of money (*i.e.,* the gold and silver and other metals), in the realm of the mother. This reminds me of what Jung had said were the three "M's" of analysis: *mother, matter,* and *money.* We see it here in this dramatic image of matter being minted into money in the temple of the mother.

The word *moneta* is from an older word, *moneo* meaning "to remind," "to put in mind," "to recollect," "to admonish," "to advise," "to warn," "to instruct," "to teach." One can see in this word *moneo* Mnemosyne at work as goddess of memory and reminding. In her role as Juno Moneta, Juno was a great advisor and seer. She could see the future. A temple was built in her honor because she warned the populace about an impending earthquake. So dwelling within the word ''money'' are images of remembering, advising, warning, and the sense of teaching and instructing through remembering the past. Forgetting to pay one's bill, or forgetting to discuss the fee, may now be seen as part of the phenomenology of money in its character as memory. Juno must get her due if something is not remembered, and we are all aware of the kind of retribution Juno dealt. Forgetting about money, not learning from money, not heeding the warnings of money, are forgetting about Juno.

The root of *moneo* was *men* which gave rise to the Latin words *memini, mens,* and *mentio. Memini* means ''to remember,'' ''to recollect,'' ''to think of,'' ''to be mindful,'' and ''to mention a thing.'' Again we are reminded of images of remembering, of filling up the mind with a thing. If money comes out of such a verbal nest, we must attend to this extraordinary emphasis on remembering and on memory. In this regard it is perhaps telling that so little is remembered, so little mentioned about money in the literature of our field and, most likely, in the offices of our practice.

Mens is a feminine noun from this root and means ''mind,'' ''heart,'' and ''soul.'' Only later was it constricted into referring to conscience and later still limited to the intellectual faculties of reason and rationality. In its personified form, *Mens* was the Roman goddess of thought. Imagine that, a *goddess* of thought! But other goddesses live here too. This root *mens* gives birth to the name Minerva, the Roman goddess of wisdom, of reflection, of arts, sciences and poetry, and of weaving.

Other words developing out of this basic root, such as *monitor, mentor, monitum,* and *monitus,* all convey images of reminding, warning and admonishing, as well as referring to these effects through oracles, omens and prophecies. Certainly images of prophecy, omens, and warnings are alive and well in relation to money. The stock markets of the world quicken with prophecy, portent, and prediction. Money advisors are full of warnings, admonitions, advice. Juno Moneta is at work here.

These images were already existent in earlier Greek times. The general Greek word for money, *chrimatos,* refers also to an oracular response and a divine warning. Thus, in all of these considerations and reflections on the images at the root of the word "money," we come to some basic connection among money, memory, and mantic practices. We have arrived at this connection through a study only of the history and origins of the word "money" and without benefit of psychological theory or praxis. I take this to mean that if we are to have a complete understanding of our relation to money in our psychological practice as well as in our understanding of money phenomena on a larger scale, we shall have to bring to bear on such reflections the intricate web of connections among money, memory and mantic practices that resides in the forgotten but still living depths of the word "money."

What is to be found in the depths of the word "self"? Its roots reach down to *seu-,* a marvelously rich element that goes into such words as "sibling," "gossip," "secret," "seduce," "suicide," "custom," and "hetaera." There isn't time to take up all these images in relation to our theme of money as a talisman of the Self. But the fact that "secret" and "self" involve the same root brings to mind how secretive we are about money. It is easier to find out which analysts are sleeping with patients than it is to find out the fee for this analytical conjunctio! It seems to me we can talk openly about sexual affairs—ours or others—but money affairs are still shrouded in secrecy. I wonder if the Self works less now in sexual affairs than in money matters. Why is it we are so secretive about money? Why do we have such trouble talking and telling about our relationship to money even with each other?

If it is true that money is a talisman of the Self, it must be that talking about money begins to reveal our relation to Self in some way that is extraordinarily real, perhaps more real than some of the other ways we more readily reveal ourselves—and perhaps more telling. Then we must consider how the word ''ethics'' mixes together with self and secret. How shall we consider the problems of money in terms of the ethics of the Self? I recall Jung's statement that insight into the nature of one's own images must be converted into an ethical obligation, and that a man's ''Failure to understand them, or a shirking of ethical responsibility, deprives him of his wholeness and imposes a painful fragmentariness on his life.''[7] Images of money and our dealing with money both in our practice and in our everyday life cannot escape this ethical binding. As can be seen from the word-work, *self, ethics* and *secret* are intertwined. I see now that the deeper purpose of secrecy is not to cover up what ego wants to hide, but to bring the ego into connection with the Self where, in secret, it comes to learn of its ethical obligations.

Ego's unconsciousness heals frequently through revelation and telling of secrets. But the secret connection with Self is revealed not through telling but through *enactment* of ethical obligations learned and remembered in secret consort with the Self. And to the extent that these reflections bear on our relation to money, what we *do* with money, more than what we *say* about money, reveals the full reality of our ethical relation to Self.

It is this *ethical relation to Self* that binds us together as a community. It is what we promise ourselves, each other, and those who seek our help. What we do with the fruits of our soul work—that hard cold cash—has much to tell us about our relation to Self, our

22

relation to telos, our relation to the ''necessities of soul.'' This money comes to us marked, marked with the soul struggles of the 'other.' It does not come clean, but bloodied in the enormous battles of another's soul. ''Money is another kind of blood,'' and when it circulates through our hands it comes perhaps with more than we care to know.

III

''Your safe deposit box is empty.'' This dream voice had so affected my patient that he rushed to the bank and checked his various safe deposit boxes. Nothing was missing. He was enormously relieved, but he was deeply troubled by the dream. He talked about having lost some inner valuables. I reminded him that he had never experienced a sense of inner values, that all his feeling and life were tied up in making money and wielding its power. It wasn't that anything was lost; it simply had never been there, and therefore the box stands empty. Sometimes when a word strikes me strongly I will work in the moment with it. I took the dictionary and simply said the images listed under the word ''empty'':

Void of content
Containing nothing
No occupants, no inhabitants
No load, no cargo
Lacking purpose, lacking substance
Idle
Needing nourishment
Hungry
Devoid and destitute
Empty.

My saying the word's meanings in this way, slowly and with feeling, brought tears to the eyes of the dreamer. The words had pierced him and brought feeling in the form of tears. When I told him that the word "empty" comes from an Old English word meaning "rest" and "leisure," he understood immediately the emptiness of his leisured life.

The Indo-European root for empty is *mod*, a root meaning "to take appropriate measures." It was time, I said, to take appropriate measures. A Latin word arising from this root is *mederi*, meaning "to look after, heal, cure," which is the source of the words "medicine" and "remedy." It seemed a bit peculiar that a word such as "empty" should belong to the same verbal nest as a word meaning "heal" and "cure." I said the medicine, the remedy, must lie in the emptiness—right there in that empty safe deposit box.

Another word from this root is the Latin *meditari* which means "to think about," "consider deeply," "reflect." It is the origin of our word "meditate." The word asks the dreamer to meditate and reflect on the emptiness. Another word from this nest is the Latin *modus* meaning "measure," "limit," "manner," "harmony," "melody." His analytic work must be a taking measure of himself, finding his limits, finding his manner, finding the harmony and melody in his life. It was all there in the emptiness. The English words mode, model, modern, modify, mold, commode, commodious, and commodity come from this Latin parent.

He meditated on the empty safe deposit box. Not much happened because he was not used to such introspective effort. That night he had a dream in which a young waif came up to him while he was getting into his limousine. The waif said: "I'll find it for a penny." The dreamer reached into his pocket and, pulling out a roll of bills, handed the boy a fifty-dollar bill. "No," said the waif, "for a penny." But neither the dreamer nor his chauffeur had a penny and the boy ran off. The dreamer woke in a panic.

Here is the typical fairytale motif of the worthless thing having the greatest value. But I focused on the more subtle theme that it was the *coin* that was required to set in motion the search for "it." The dreamer understood "it" to be his connection to soul without which his fortune had become meaningless. It was the way, the remedy, the medicine for the emptiness.

I have long since felt it necessary, when dealing with dreams in which money images occur, to focus first on the actuality of the dreamer's relation to money. What about pennies? The dreamer revealed that he had a long-standing habit of rejecting pennies in any transaction. He simply would not accept pennies as change. In pursuing why he rejected pennies, we discovered that it was not because they were of so little value (as the fairytale motif would have led us to believe), but because they were *copper*. He would only accept the silvery coins as change. I understood, at least empathically, because my own childhood box of coins would never admit pennies. They had to be silver. The man, hating copper, was hating the very metal necessary for him to find his way to soul.

He could not remember what had set him so against copper, so against pennies. He spoke, too, of feeling that if he did accept pennies something terrible would happen. He warded off such fears by scrupulously continuing not to touch pennies. Right here is that web of interconnections among money, memory and mantic practices of which I spoke earlier. One can see clearly how this man's fate is intricately bound up with these coins, how the penny is required as a fee for finding connection to soul, and how his relation to copper produces the emptiness of incompleteness; how this "turn of events" turned him, and how the ironic "twist" of a rich man not having a penny confronted him with his destiny, sending him into a writhing worry.

As ever, I was intrigued by the word "copper." It is, of course, the Latin *cuprum* from an earlier Greek word which was the name of the Island of Cyprus. This is the source of the best copper in ancient times. The name Cyprus is thought to derive from a Hebrew word, *gopher*, the name of the tree whose wood was used to make the ark. It was this image that released the repressed memory of the priest slapping his hands as he tried to steal from the offering plate the few pennies that had been left there. The priest, too, liked silver best.

A patient, accustomed to paying me with a check at the beginning of each hour, was writing one out, an activity usually performed in silence. He said, ''Well, what happened to you this week?'' I suddenly found myself unable to remember anything about my week. I was struggling to remember something when he said, ''No, wait until I give you this. The gods might not like it if we begin before I pay.'' Clearly, for this patient, the payment had to do not just with me but with the gods. And although he said this in a joking manner, I listened as well to its serious purpose. The payment was a mantic offering to propitiate the gods and to secure their good counsel. He handed me the check, which, although made out to me, was for the gods. What is one to do with such an offering? Something accepted as part of a sacred ritual ought to be used for sacred purposes. Isn't this one of the ways money would consecrate the work? I began to puzzle over what particular use I could put this money to. I wondered if spending this money on something other than a sacred purpose would in some way affect the process engaging us. By the end of the hour I had forgotten my musings, put his check together with the others, and sent them all to the bank.

We often work diligently to keep our patients separate, often going to elaborate extremes so that no patient sees another, so that no trace of a previous patient is left in the office. But we do not hesitate to commingle our patients' money. The connection between the *origin* of the money and the *fate* of the money is broken by putting the money in a common, undifferentiated pool. This also keeps us from attending to the connection between what our patient has given us and what we do with it.

Did it really matter how I spent this money? I realized at once that this bit of consciousness—or was it a crazy romanticism—would make it exceedingly difficult blindly to deposit all those checks each month into an undifferentiated pool of money. I realized I was going to be plagued by this image of money carrying something of the soul of my patients and by the notion that how I use the money may affect not only my own soul but theirs as well. Something kept shouting, "It doesn't matter, it doesn't matter." But now I couldn't believe that. It must matter in some way. "Silliness," the voices chorused.

Well, perhaps. But suppose our patients paid us not in checks, not even in cash, but in goods and services as in former times. Then the eggs you ate would be those brought by that hysterical woman, the cloth that made your pants brought by that depressive who can't get into life; your roof would be fixed by that alcoholic who beats his wife, and your garden planted by that woman with that terrible erotic transference. Now all of this leads into the most fantastic issues. From this point of view, dissolving our patients' money into some common pool—which breaks the connection between the money and what we do with it—allows us to remain unconscious of these things.

Recently, a psychotherapist consulted me concerning a problem he couldn't resolve. He was married with a stable family life, but for a variety of reasons found himself involved with another woman. His problem was not particularly a conflict about this extramarital relationship—he was not experiencing any difficulties about this. His problem was one of money. His other woman was expensive, and he had fallen into supporting her—paying her rent, buying clothes, and so on. He had pictured himself as perhaps worth more than he was. And, for a time, there was no difficulty. But now the ever increasing costs of this affair were becoming onerous, and he couldn't find any way to cut down or reduce them. He became depressed, which usually meant he spent even more on her as a way of alleviating the depression. The distress of these escalating expenses brought him to analysis.

After listening attentively to this tale for a while, I asked him who was paying for this affair. He was, of course. And where did the money come from? Well, almost all of his income was from his private practice. We then discussed the actual amounts that were being paid to support the other woman. They ranged between $1,000 and $1,500 a month and rising. I asked him to imagine the exact source of this money. He didn't understand. He paid it from cash, savings, and his checking account. Yes, I said, but these monies have an exact source. Patient A pays you $400 a month, patient B $200 a month and so on. These are the concrete sums that come from individual people in your practice. Could you specify which of your patients are paying for this affair?

He became quite angry, accused me of moralizing and trying to induce guilt. I didn't argue. After he calmed down I simply repeated the question.

I had not known why I put the question in this way. I do know that the art of analysis often is finding the right question. I don't know that this was the right question. But as I was speaking to him my own mind was racing into my own financial dealings and putting the question to myself. I had only just begun to consider a possible link between what a patient pays me and what I do with it afterward. I had been sufficiently schooled in how to treat and relate to all manner of patient attitudes, feelings, and behavior about money. But no one had mentioned to me that what I did with this money might be of some genuine significance in the work.

Imagine that the money we receive from a patient carries something of that patient's soul or psyche or value or energy. This money personifies the patient, and as I have described earlier carries something of the patient's telos, the patient's fate. The money is a substance, a metal, a coin, a transformative talisman that is passed into our hands in payment for our time, our energy, our love, our value. Is consciousness required of us as analysts to examine how we treat this money? Does the fate of this money have an impact on the analytic process? You have a mortgage payment due next month. Or maybe some secret diversion requires money. Could you consciously choose which of your patients' money to use in this way? Clearly, it is easier to break all connection between individual patients and the payment of our own expenses. That we do by mixing together all our patients' money. But *could* we make such decisions? On what basis would such decisions be made? Or would it be better to keep this entire possibility unconscious and not intermix the fate of our patients' money so intricately and individually into our personal life? But this is just a mask. We cannot avoid mixing our patients into our personal life, because the financial foundation of our personal life—at least for most of us—is built by our patients. While this question raises such enormous difficulties, there isn't time to deal adequately with them. I must be satisfied with simply raising the issue. And, besides, like any good analytic hour, the time is up at just the critical moment, leaving us not with answers but, I hope, with pregnant questions.

1. Simon Macdonald Lockhart, *Seven Centuries: The History of the Lockharts of Lee and Carnwath* (privately published by S.F. Macdonald Lockhart, Estate Office, Carnwath, Lanark, Scotland, 1977), p. 8.

2. Edward F. Edinger, *Melville's Moby Dick: A Jungian Commentary* (New

York: New Directions, 1978), p. 107.

3. Herman Melville, *Moby Dick; or The Whale* (Chicago: Encyclopedia Britannica, 1971), p. 317.

4. As cited by H. L. Mencken, *A New Dictionary of Quotations* (New York: Alfred A. Knopf, 1977), p. 804.

5. As cited in Gaston Bachelard, *The Poetics of Reverie* (Boston: Beacon Press, 1971), p. 48.

6. Russell A. Lockhart, "Words as Eggs," *Dragonflies* I/i (1978), p. 30.

7. C. G. Jung, *Memories, Dreams, Reflections* (New York: Vintage Books, 1963), p. 193.

A Contribution to Soul and Money

By James Hillman

"Money is a kind of poetry"
Wallace Stevens, "Adagia"
Opus Posthumous, 1957

Whatever we say about money in its relation with analytical practice, whatever we say about money at all will be conditioned by the
mind-set of our cultural tradition. We speak first of all at an un-
reflected level, with the voice of collective consciousness, to use
Jung's term. So, in order to gain purchase on the money question in
analysis, we have first to see through our collective consciousness,
the very deep, old, and imperceptible attitudes that archetypally, let
us say, have money already fixed within a definite framework,
especially in regard to soul.

This framework is that of our entire culture, and it is Christian.
So we are going to have to look first of all at Christian ideas and im-
ages regarding money and soul. I set forth now without benefit of
Christian apologetics and exegetics, without recourse to scholarly

31

apparatus, simply as the plain man who opens his Bible in a hotel room and takes the words there within the framework of his collective consciousness. For the words of Jesus in regard to money, whether or not we are directly conscious of them, are still sounding in us as members of this culture. Here are a few of the passages in the Gospels which I want briefly to remind you of before drawing some conclusions.

John's Gospel puts the first of these money stories at the beginning of Jesus' ministry (John 2:14).

> And he found in the temple those that sold oxen and sheep and doves, and the changers of money sitting [*kollubistes*, literally "coin clippers"]. And he made a scourge of cords and cast all out of the temple, both the sheep and the oxen; and he poured out the changers' money, and overthrew their tables. And to them that sold the doves he said, Take these things hence; Make not my Father's house a house of merchandise [a market].

Mark's (11:17) version has Jesus saying "a den of robbers," specifically referring to both buyers and sellers.

The second incident is more a saying than a story. I refer to Matthew 19, Mark 10, and Luke 8:25 from which last I quote: "For it is easier for a camel to enter in through a needle's eye, than for a rich man to enter into the kingdom of heaven." Is it not curious that in these first two allegories money is expressed directly in the language of animals? Even the sheep and oxen, so significant in the birth milieu of Jesus, are driven from the temple, and the camel now becomes that animal fatness, that richness which cannot pass the strait and narrow gate where the soul must enter. In these first two images, the exclusion of money is also exclusion of the animal.

If ever the word archetypal meant anything like permanent, ubiquitous, at the roots or made in heaven, then the relation between money and animals is archetypal. The animal is the very archai of money. Pecuniary derives from cattle; fee derives from *faihi* (Gothic for cattle); capital refers back to cattle counted by the head. The Greek coin, *obolos*, refers to the *obelos* or spitted portion of flesh of a sacrificial bull, and the ancient Roman currency, *as*, meant a piece of the roast, a hunk of meat.* The vow of poverty entails the vow of chastity; money and animal life are driven from the temple together.

The third story concerns taxes, which play a special role right from the beginning. Jesus' birth took place in Bethlehem because Joseph and Mary had to proceed there to register for the tax rolls (Luke 2). The topos, "Bethlehem," not only brings Jesus together with David, Jesus and animal together, Joseph and Mary together, the Magi of various races and orientations, but also holds in one image the Emperor's rule of the world by means of taxes and Christ's star pointing beyond the world. In the image of "Bethlehem," as they say, no problem. In Matthew 17 (and Matthew, by the way, is the Patron Saint of tax collectors, assessors and bankers), Peter is asked whether Jesus pays his half-shekel or didrachma in taxes. Peter says: Yes. But as it turns out, the tax Jesus pays to the Temple is not common money of this world. It is got by miracle: "go thou to the sea," he tells Simon Peter, ". . . and take up the fish that first cometh up; and when thou hast opened his mouth, thou shalt find a shekel: take that and give unto them for me and thee." Again, by the way, an animal together with money.

The main tax tale is the one told in Matthew 22, Mark 12, and Luke 20. I'll give the passage from Mark: "Master . . . is it lawful to give tribute unto Caesar, or not?" to which Jesus answers: "bring me a penny that I may see it . . . And he saith unto them, Whose is this image and superscription? And they said unto him, Caesar's. And Jesus said unto them, Render unto Caesar the things

*Cf. W.H. Desmonde, *Magic, Myth, and Money* (Glencoe: Free Press), pp. 109-19.

that are Caesar's, and unto God the things that are God's.''

Here it is money itself which divides into two alternative ways—spiritual and worldly. It is money which is used for the parable of two different and distinct worlds. If money divides the two realms, is it also that third which holds them together? We shall come to this later.

According to the texts, it sounds as if it is clearly better to be without money, even to be in poverty, than to be with money. (This in spite of Joseph of Arimethea and other followers who were wealthy.) For instance, in the tale of the poor widow (Luke 20, Mark 12) who is praised for her meager giving—a lesson Jesus draws out for his disciples as he sits ''over against the treasury'' in the temple. Or, for instance, poverty becomes mandatory: when the twelve are sent on their mission, two by two, with authority over unclean spirits or *daimones* (Mark 6, Luke 9, Matthew 10), they are expressly instructed not to carry money. Or, for instance, Luke 12 where wealth and soul are directly brought into relation. In a passage about inheritance (the parable of the rich fool) Jesus says: ''a man's life consisteth not in the abundance of things which he possesseth'' as he tells about a rich man laying up corn for his retirement so as to have his soul's ease, only to have his same soul (psyche) called by God to death that very night. Or, for instance, Matthew 26 and Mark 8: ''What doth it profit a man to gain the whole world and lose his own soul [psyche]?''

Is not by now the division utterly clear? Money belongs to Caesar's Palace, not God's Temple. The first act of cleansing the temple of money is reaffirmed all along, and of course nowhere more bitterly than in the final story, the selling of Jesus by Judas for thirty pieces of silver. (Judas is already attributed with the telltale sign of evil—a money bag or box in the scene of the supper [John 13:29].) Could money be given a more negative cast?

34

We are situated in this collective consciousness. We have to start from this schism between soul and money in the basic text stating the values of our tradition. The schism can lead us into taking up one side or another of it, such as exposed by Dr. Covitz and by Dr. Vasavada. Together with Vasavada, we can deny money in order to do a spiritual kind of soul-work; or together with Covitz, we can affirm money in order to become therapeutically more effective in the world. They each showed the division we already have seen: (the more one concentrates on money the more one involves oneself in the world, and the more one neglects money or abjures it, the more one can be removed from the world.

But I wish to make another kind of move by taking a third position, neither high road nor low road, neither spirit nor matter. I see money as an archetypal dominant that can be taken spiritually or materially, but which in itself is neither.

Rather, money is a *psychic reality*, and as such gives rise to divisions and oppositions about it, much as other fundamental psychic realities—love and work, death and sexuality, politics and religion—are archetypal dominants which easily fall into opposing spiritual and material interpretations. Moreover, since money is an archetypal psychic reality, it will always be inherently problematic because psychic realities are complex, complicated. Therefore, money problems are inevitable, necessary, irreducible, always present, and potentially if not actually overwhelming. Money is devilishly divine.

One of Charles Olson's *Maximus* poems sets out this archetypal view most compactly:

> the under part is, though stemmed, uncertain is, as sex is, 'as moneys are,
> facts to be dealt with as the sea is . . .

This is an extraordinary statement. ''Facts to be dealt with as the

35

sea is.'' The first of these facts is that money is as deep and broad as the ocean, the primordially unconscious, and makes us so. It always takes us into great depths, where sharks and suckers, hard-shell crabs, tight clams and tidal emotions abound. Its facts have huge horizons, as huge as sex, and just as protean and polymorphous.

Moreover, money is plural: money*s*. Therefore I can never take moneys as an equivalent for any single idea: exchange, energy, value, reality, evil, and whatever. It is many-stemmed, it is uncertain, polymorphous. At one moment the money complex may invite Danae who draws Zeus into her lap as a shower of coins, at another moment the gold may invite Midas. Or, Hermes the thief, patron of merchants, easy commerce. Or it may be old moneybags Saturn who invented coining and hoarding to begin with. As on the original coins the Greeks made, there are different Gods and different animals—owls, bulls, rams, crabs—each time the complex is passed from hand to hand.

Money is as protean as the sea-God himself; try as we might with fixed fees, regular billings, and accounts ledgered and audited, we never can make the stems of money balance. The checkbook will never tally, the budget will never stay within bookkeeping columns. We invent more and more machinery for controlling money, more and more refined gauges for economic prediction, never grasping what Olson tells us: the facts of money are like the facts of the sea. Money is like the id itself, the primordially repressed, the collective unconscious appearing in specific denominations, that is, precise quanta or configurations of value, i.e., *images*. Let us define money as that which possibilizes the imagination. Moneys are the riches of Pluto in which Hades' psychic images lie concealed. To find imagination in yourself or a patient, turn to money behaviors and fantasies. You both will soon be in the underworld (the entrance to which requires a money for Charon).

JAMES HILLMAN

Therapy draws back. Do you know of the study done on therapeutic taboos? Analysts were surveyed regarding what they feel
they must never do with a patient. It was discovered that touching
and holding, shouting and hitting, drinking, kissing, nudity and in-
tercourse were all less prohibited than was ''lending money to a patient.'' Money constellated the ultimate taboo.

For money always takes us into the sea, uncertain, whether it
comes as inheritance fights, fantasies about new cars and old houses,
marriage battles over spending, ripping off, tax evasion, market
speculations, fear of going broke, poverty, charity—whether these
complexes appear in dreams, in living rooms, or in public policy. For
here in the facts of money is the great ocean, and maybe while trawl-
ing that sea floor during an analytical hour we may come up with a
crazy crab or a fish with a shekel in its mouth.

Just as animals were spirits or Gods in material forms, so too is
money, a kind of third thing between only spirit and only the world,
flesh, and devil. Hence, to be with money is to be in this third place
of soul, psychic reality. And, to keep my relation with the unclean
spirits whether the high daimones or the low daimones, I want some
coins in my purse. I need them to pay my way to Hades into the
psychic realm. I want to be like what I work on, not unlike and im-
mune. I want the money-changers where I can see them, right in the
temple of my pious aspirations. In other words, I try my darndest to
keep clear about the tradition I have just exposed because I think it a
disastrous one for psychotherapy, and of course also for the culture
as a whole.

The cut between Caesar and God in terms of money deprives the
soul of world and the world of soul. The soul is deflected onto a
spiritual path of denial and the world is left in the sins of luxuria,
avarice, and greed. Then the soul is always threatened by money,
and the world needs the spiritual mission of redemption from the

37

evil caused by the Weltbild that cuts Caesar from God. That money
is the place where God and Caesar divide shows that money is a
'third thing' like the soul itself, and that in money are both the inherent tendency to split into spirit and matter and the possibility to
hold them together.

This equation—"money = psyche"—is what we Jungians have
been trying to say when we translate money images in dreams into
"psychic energy." "Energy," however, is heroic Promethean
language. It transforms the equation into "money = ego," that is,
energy available to ego-consciousness. Then, Hermes/Mercurius,
Guide of Souls, has to appear as the thief, and in our sense of loss (of
money, of energy, of identity) in order for the equation "money =
psyche" to return again. (Poverty is simply a way out of ego, but
not a hermetic way.) For Hermes the Thief is also Hermes Psycho-
pompos, implying that from the hermetic perspective exactly there,
where money is no longer available to ego-consciousness, is also
where Hermes has stolen it for the sake of soul. In soul work, losing
and gaining take on different meanings, a sensibility that Promethean language about "energy" is too active and goal-directed to
apprehend.

If money has this archetypal soul value, again like the ancient
coins bearing images of Gods and their animals and backed by these
powers,* money will not, cannot, accept the Christian depreciation,
and so Christianity time and again in its history has had to come to
terms with the return of the repressed—from the wealth of the
churches and the luxury of its priests, the selling of indulgences, the
rise of capitalism with protestantism, usury and projections on the
Jews, the Christian roots of marxism, and so on.

One particular shadow of the Christian position appears right in

*Cf. my discussion of coinage in "Silver and the White Earth," *Spring 1980*, pp. 35-37.

analysis: the old sin of *simony* or exchanging spiritual and ec-
clesiastical benefits for money. Is not the elaborate system analysts
have derived for guaranteed payments from their patients for 'Heil'
or individuation of the Self, and from their trainees for ordination into the analytical profession, modern forms of simony? This sin the
Church was far more conscious of than we are today. The Church
was anyway more aware of money for possibilizing the imagination
than we are in psychotherapy. It has always recognized the fantasy-
power of money preventing the soul from its doctrinal spiritual path.

As long as our belief system inherently depreciates money, it will
always threaten the soul with value distortions. Depression, inflation, bad credit, low interest—these psychological metaphors have
hardened into unconscious economic jargon. Having "de-based"
money from its archetypal foundations in psychic reality, money attempts a new literal and secular foundation for itself as "the bottom
line." But this bottom does not hold, because any psychic reality
that has been fundamentally depreciated must become symptomatic,
'go crazy,' in order to assert its fundamental archetypal autonomy.

We live today in fear of this autonomy, called financial anarchy.
Anarchy means "without archai"; and of course money, conceived
without soul, without an animal life of its own, without Gods, becomes crazy, anarchic, because we forget that like sex, like the sea, it
too is a religious dominant.

Now I am referring back through the word itself to the Goddess
Moneta, the Roman equivalent of Mnemosyne meaning *memoria,*
imaginatio, Mother of the Muses. In her temple of Moneta, money
was kept; in the word, a temple too, Moneta reappears. Money is
thus a deposit of mythical fantasies. It is a treasury that mothers and
remembers images. Money is imaginative, as I have been saying.
Thus, money in the hand awakens imaginal possibilities: to do this,
go there, have that. It reveals the Gods which dominate my fan-

tasies—Saturnian tightness, Jupiterian generosity, Martial show, Venusian sensuality. Money provokes my behavior into mythical fantasies, so very different in different people. Why should people agree about money—where to invest it, on what to spend it, which horse to put it on? It is a truly polytheistic phenomenon in everyday life. As such, coined money is a highly cultural phenomenon. It came into history with the Greeks and not before them. It belongs in the constellation of the Muses, necessary to imaginational culture, and hence it does become devilish when imagination is not valued (as in Christianity). The ugliness, the power corruption, the purely quantitative nature of money today are not its fault, but that of its having been severed and then fallen from the Gods from which it came.

*

Let me now connect this theme with another at this Congress: Training. On occasion candidates have explained to me that one reason for their wanting to train is that analytical practice offers a noble way of earning money. So much of the world's work is soul-less, they say, while analysis pays one for staying with soul, without having to open a headshop, teach guitar, throw pots or home-grow squash and tomatoes. One does not have to be economically marginal. The analyst combines soul and money; analytical money is good, clean money, and even well paid. Training tempts, evidently, because it resolves the Christian dilemma of shekel versus soul, without having to follow the spiritual solution of poverty.

The resolution of a pair of opposites, however, only perpetuates their opposition: the third requires the other two for it to be a third. Only when we can step altogether out of the dilemma that divides money (and soul) into spiritual and material oppositions, can we see that there is psyche in money all the time in every way, that it is ''a kind of poetry,'' that it is wholly and utterly psychological and needs no redeeming into good, clean and noble money, and so needs no repressing into the poverty and asceticism of the spirit turned against matter.

In fact, that equation "money = psyche" suggests that there is more soul to be found where money problems are most extreme, not in poverty but in luxury, miserly greed, covetousness, and the joy of usury, and that the fear of money and the importance of money in some persons may be more psychologically devastating, and therefore therapeutically rewarding, than sexual fears and impotence. Extraordinary demons are startled when the money complex is touched. And no complex is kept hidden with more secrecy. Patients more readily reveal what's concealed by their pants than what's hidden in their pants' pockets. Freudians who see purses as female genital symbols may discover more by making the reduction in the reverse direction.

Where exactly is the money complex hidden? Most often it hides in the guises of love, where so much soul is anyways hidden. As Tawney showed, Protestantism and Capitalism enter the world together. And, after all these centuries, they still hold hands in mutual affection in so many protestant families where giving, receiving, saving, participating, supporting, spending, willing (inheritance) are the ways one learns about loving. "Spending" for a long time in English had both a genital and a monetary meaning, while the words bond, yield, safe, credit, duty, interest, share and debt (as *schuld* or guilt) all bear double meanings of love and money. The double meanings double-bind: to protestant-capitalist consciousness renunciating the family's psychological attitudes often becomes refusing money from home which is felt at home as a rebuff of love. The money = psyche equation is a powerful variant of the Eros and Psyche myth where money stands in for love.

But finally, what does money do for the soul: what is its specific function in possibilizing the imagination? It makes the imagination possible in the world. Soul needs money to be kept from flying off into the Bardo realm of 'only-psychic' reality. Money holds soul in the vale of the world, in the poetry of the concrete, in touch with the sea as *facts*, those hard and slippery facts, so perduring, annoying, and limiting, and ceaselessly involving one in economic necessity. For economy means originally "householding," making soul in the vale of the world, charging and being overcharged, crimping and splurging, exchanging, bargaining, evaluating, paying off, going in debt, speculating . . . .

Thus fee negotiation, whether in Vasavada's style or Covitz's, is a thoroughly psychological activity. Fee payment may take many styles from dirty dollar bills plunked on the table before the hour begins, to gifts and deals and wheedling, or the discreetly passed envelope, to the abstract medical model of depersonalized forms, checks, and statements. And the old joke is always true: "When the man says: 'it ain't the money, it's the principle'—it's the money." It *is* the money where the real issue lies. Money is an irreducible principle.

Analysis, as the candidates have perceived, indeed lets soul and money meet. The spirituality of the Christian division is suspended: one renders unto the Gods and Caesars in one and the same payment. We pay tribute to the costliness of soul work, that it is rare, precious, most dear. And we pay out the common buck "for professional services rendered," a phrase equally appropriate to the physician, the plumber, and the whore.

That analysts have trouble justifying their outrageous fees (and at the same time feel they never earn enough compared with lawyers and dentists) belongs to the archetypal nature of money as we have been viewing it. The money question can no more be regulated so as to settle into easiness than can sex or the sea. The underpart stems into the many directions of our complexes. That we cannot settle the money issue in analysis shows money to be one main way the mothering imagination keeps our souls fantasizing. So, to conclude with my part of this panel, Soul and Money: yes, soul *and* money; we cannot have either without the other. To find the soul of modern man or woman, begin by searching into those irreducible embarrassing facts of the money complex, that crazy crab scuttling across the floors of silent seas.

Fee-Less Practice and Soul Work

By Arwind Vasavada

When I started to work in the States in 1970 as a Jungian analyst, I found it difficult to talk about fees when an analysand inquired about them. It felt strange to equate a fixed sum of money with whatever happened in the session. After all, what was the fee for? That hour? My person? His need to pay? Was he in fact buying something or was he exchanging money for work done? If it was an exchange of money for work, then what was the criterion for deciding the amount of money—time on the clock, a quality of work? If the second, then the fee must change each hour, assessing it according to the value of that particular hour. When the hour went well, there was no problem, but often times the sessions were less illuminating and helpful, they depressed me, and I could see the depression in the face of the client as well.

The question would not let me go. Can payment for work be considered an installment purchase? If so, then it belonged to a long-term contract for work supposed to be done. But can one guarantee in advance the quality of work according to an agreed-upon fee? Perhaps the criterion for payment is biological security; a fee simply takes care of human needs. Once again the problem gets complicated. How much do I need? There is no limit. I want all the comforts and luxuries others have, and I feel I deserve them as others do.

While living in India on a fixed salary from the University, it was a simple matter. I adjusted my needs and wants to fit within that sum. But here I became aware of my greed, and I liked it. When in Rome . . . . I soon felt comfortable with this idea, and made good progress with work and money. I could rent a reasonably good apartment and have a car. In 1972 I returned to India for the first time since I started work in the States. During this trip I visited my Guru, the blind saint.

Through letters and talks when we met, he must have been aware of whatever was going on in my life. He asked me how long I would be working and if I could see a time when I could not work. Without work, what would I do? He put it very clearly, "To this day your mind and body are healthy and you can work. There will be a time when the mind will not be sharp because of age, and the body will probably be weak also. What will you do then? How would you feel without work?

Remember when you were an infant, helpless in every way. Were you not cared for? You will be cared for always if you can feel into the trust you had then as an infant. Although helpless and without work, you will not feel lost. Just be nothing. In order to be Nothing, be free from all ambitions and desires. You worked as long as you were in India—until the age of retirement. Had you stayed you would naturally have not worked anymore. So do not work where you live now, but serve instead. Don't ask for any fixed fee, accept what is given freely and happily."

I listened to all this and to all the doubts surfacing within. I was quite unclear as to how I could follow this guidance, but it did appeal to me. I promised myself to try it out. He was my Guru, a person blind since the age of ten, uneducated, sixty years old—perhaps more than seventy—and without house, bags or baggage.

This conversation reminded me of my experience with my first Guru. Then I had received, though I had not paid. My first Guru was a family man. He did not, however, work to support himself; his only source of income was whatever he was offered. Yet he came some 1500 miles from his home to see me whenever I asked, and also spent sums of money to entertain me adequately whenever I visited his home. I knew I had paid him hardly anything.

By the time I came to this country, I had realized that the way of Jung and the tradition of my Gurus were alike. The work was Soul Work, Soul Making. This country gave me the opportunity to fulfill this possibility within myself and to do Soul Work with others. However, only when I visited my Guru in 1972 did I realize that Soul Work is not a professional work for money.

Upon my return to the States, I began to change. When a client asked about my fees, I told him that I would be glad to receive whatever was given gladly. "Give me happily and freely whatever you can conveniently and without constraint." If the patient asked about the fees charged by my colleagues, I informed him about the present rate.

The discussion with my Guru returned me to my Soul Work, and it felt truly in line with the way of Jung. If Jung's way is to explore the Unknown and to live with the uncertainty and unpredictability of the Unconscious, then living with the uncertainty of flexible fees seems to be the way to experience what Jung said and taught.

During this period I was paid only what people felt happy in giving. A few could not pay; a few paid five or ten dollars, and some paid the full fee. Others offered to do work, such as cleaning, altering clothes, or making a bookcase.

What is the effect of the fee-less practice on the patient? In the absence of fees, is commitment to the work possible? I see no connection between exchange of money and commitment to work together. The person comes to therapy suffering and in pain. One listens to it, feels it; naturally the heart goes out to do whatever possible. While feeling this way, can one throw out the suffering person simply because he cannot pay the *reasonable* fee? Commitment to work is obvious, since here is an opportunity to enter the temple of the healing God. In my experience people have always paid what they could; therapy did not stop as insight and image went on gracing the hour. I can remember only one solitary case when a client cheated me.

Another example shows that sensitivity can grow during the work, while people pay happily. A person from the healing professions agreed to pay a certain sum in the beginning. Later, after a month or so, he felt the exchange of money was interfering with the work. I told him that if he thought not paying would make him comfortable and flowing in the work, then I was happy about that too. We continued for some time. Following his return from a vacation he told me that he gave some amount to a charity, and felt good about it. The work commenced again until he left the state on a work assignment. When he came back, he felt happy in paying me for each session. This illustrates how contract in terms of money is not essential to Soul Work.

Some misunderstanding may lurk here. This kind of fee-less practice does not mean that the therapist is unaware of the client's sense of obligation for what he is receiving. Such a lacuna is detrimental to both analyst and client. The common and reasonable understanding that one must pay for services rendered cannot be ignored. But this need not imply insistence on payment of a fixed sum of money. One who wishes to get help without paying for it deprives himself from receiving by the very nature of his attitude. He is cutting himself off from the mainstream of Life. Life is an interdependent and inter-related whole. Such a person becomes isolated from the world, ceasing to be nourished, renewed and replenished by Life. He has ceased to participate in the *Yajna*, sacrifice, of Life. Life is *Yajna*, as beautifully described by Sri Krishna in the *Gita*.

When Arjuna asks him why he is now being asked to act—fight in the battle—since Sri Krishna has already said that the path of knowledge is better than the path of action, Sri Krishna says Non-action may not be achieved by ceasing to act or by renunciation of acts. Without action human beings will die (*Bh. Gita*, III 4-5). It is here that Krishna introduces the concept of action as *Yajna*. In a very symbolic way he explains how this universe is sustained by *Yajna*.

He says: Everything grows and is sustained by food. Food is produced by rain, and *Yajna* performed brings rain. In order to perform *Yajna* one must act and work, gathering material to be sacrificed in the fire of *Yajna* (*Bh. Gita*, III 14-16). The common understanding that one can choose between action and non-action is incorrect. Sri Krishna says that the source of action is Brahman, the totality of what IS; since this totality is established in the Immutable *(Akshara)*, everything returns to and originates from the same source. We are nourished and sustained by that. Performing the *Yajna*, being in the mainstream of life, sustains us. Whoever alienates himself from the fact of Life, its interdependence and mutuality, isolates himself from his own source and ceases to live. Sincerity of purpose always brings reciprocity and respect and a healing wholeness.

The experiment with the fee-less practice opened many dark corners of my psyche, and the process goes on. I have my practice as a Jungian analyst and occasionally teach Indian psychology and philosophy in a small suburban college.

As might be expected, both income and the number of clients rise and fall. One month is not the same as any other; no year resembles the one just past. I have sometimes felt acutely the impact of these fluctuations. Whenever income and clients declined, my stomach felt hollow, and a sense of insecurity pounded my heart. With pain I drew money from my savings to pay the tax collector and other bills. My insecurity intensified when such periods came regularly.

Although some years were bad, the savings balance gradually returned to its previous level. I felt very happy and even secure. As my habits are, I became something of a spendthrift. Looking back, I can say I enjoyed it, but I didn't then. This period lasted until 1977, when the sense of insecurity due to instability of income and my aging monopolized my attention.

In the summer of 1977 another and more interesting phase of life came up which had remained unnoticed and neglected until then. In the last part of August 1977 I returned from India after discharging the last responsibility to my family—seeing my youngest daughter married. A great burden was lifted from my shoulders. Since the time of my wife's death I had felt keenly the obligation to see that our pet child was married happily. Three trips to India, made in order to fulfill my responsibility, naturally affected my bank balance and clientele.

Curiously enough, the relief at her marriage and at the consequent reduction of my financial burden did not last. In its place, surreptitiously, a feeling of worthlessness and meaninglessness began to permeate my life. My responsibility for my family was at an end; it was all over. Where was the purpose of living? At the same time my knowledge, whether learned from Jung or my Gurus, began to seem hackneyed, stale and useless. All I knew left me cold, and I did not want to repeat worn-out words and feelings in analytical hours. I felt out-of-date and good-for-nothing. Existence seemed futile.

I was glad to know that the way of Jung and the path of Self-realization of the East were similar, and that the basis of psychotherapy is the knowledge and awareness of who I am. Without this awareness no help really is forthcoming in our work. Yet the soul was in agony as in a classical depression. If I knew nothing, all knowledge having departed, how would I work and live? The total uncertainty scared me. No knowledge . . . no work . . . no money . . . what then . . . ?

Something happened. Sri Shunyata (Mr. Nobody) visited me for a month. He is today ninety, comes from Denmark, and lives in a small hut in the foothills of the Himalayas on a small stipend of fifty rupees per month. In 1930 when he came to India at the invitation of Dr. Rabindranath Tagore to teach silence, he met Raman Maharshi. Raman Maharshi gazed into the eyes of Mr. Sorenson (his original name) and called him a born mystic. He said, "We are always aware, Shunyata!" In this way he was named Shunyata by Raman Maharshi.

Sri Shunyata's unobtrusive and powerfully silent personality affected me deeply. After he left, I saw some light in what had happened earlier—the classical depression.

Am I nothing if I cannot work? Am I nothing if all the acquired knowledge leaves me? What precisely is work? Is it analyzing and getting money, or is it a happening in the soul achieved through living interaction with clients and the world? The effacement of the one who could work scared me through and through.

The path I had embarked on opened innumerable fears in me until, ultimately, it led me to inquire into the root of insecurity itself. I became aware of the fact that I was identified with knowledge, a knowledge which had become the basis of my work. When knowledge had gone, security in work followed. It had been natural for me to forget myself in the doing of therapy. Once I was involved, the session hour progressed spontaneously and generally to the satisfaction of both analyst and client. Now I was nothing. I was mighty scared by the face of Nothingness. Unable to stay wholly with the experience, I could see only the nothingness of myself, while Mr. Nobody, Sri Shunyata, presented himself as a person based on Nothingness and whose work on my soul emerged not from knowledge, not even from his work, but from the soul itself. I found a new basis for soul work.

An example here to show how freedom from money (not charging a fixed fee) provides inner strength. Therapy happens between two souls when they meet honestly and sincerely—a discovery that is liberating and a relief. A client had been working with me for the last seven years. Upon retiring he reduced his appointments by half. He was a very greedy man in that, now that he had retired, he wanted a return on all the benefits of his past payments. Not at peace with himself, all alone and without work, he became impatient. No longer receiving a salary, he had only his pension and social security. At first in a veiled manner, and then plainly, he began complaining that having paid so much, not only to me, but to many others like me, he had not yet gotten what he wanted. It was my duty to give him that now.

Once in a session, he got angry and made no bones about telling me that he had been robbed. He ought now, he told me, to have peace of mind. Undisturbed by his anger, I could tell him, honestly, that I had never entered into a contract with him to supply him with this peace of mind in return for money. Calmly I told him that, although therapy happened every time we met, I never claimed to be a therapist. Nonetheless, his anger was justified. In return for his sacrifice he ought to get something. But he was angry with the wrong person. I helped him to see the healer within him, and to see through the projection of that healer onto me. This healer was the right person to be angry with. If the client really placed his complaints before Him clearly and openly, an answer was sure to come.

This brief autobiography of mine presents clearly a problem of soul work. Whether we call our work "the way to wholeness" or "a spiritual journey" or "individuation" or "soul-making," every encounter in our work with people is a two-way process, a giving and receiving, and leaves us transformed. But is this giving and receiving necessarily identical with an exchange of money? In soul work a super-ordinate factor, encompassing both analyst and client, is active. If we are open to it, it does the work. But 'who' then gets paid and 'who' pays? What is true of therapeutic work is perhaps true of all kinds of work.

Two issues here seem important to me: my uncertainty in the world and my fear of being without work. Both can result in a refusal to acknowledge the super-ordinate factor in analysis. Perhaps both meet at a common point and have a common root. Let us see.

As a biological being I am quite insecure: I need shelter, food and clothing to protect me. We all need this, yet even were this guaranteed us, life can end at any moment without notice. In spite of all care, life is beyond my control. If I worry too much about this, it is a neurotic and unhealthy fear. One must live with this insecurity, yielding to death the moment it comes.

While alive I need money to live. When I recall the periods when there was no work, no money coming in and my savings depleted by paying bills, I discover that the fear originated with the specter of not being able to maintain a certain standard of living. What is this attachment? A fear of poverty? What kind of poverty? Is it fear of poverty or love of creaturely comforts? Can I not be what I am without these comforts? Why am I here in this country doing whatever it is I am doing? Is it not because it supports my love of comforts? I know that I can be what I really am in spite of these comforts, yet a fear lurks behind it all. Deprive me of these comforts and I must face poverty. I cannot and do not want to face it.

The fear of poverty prevents the discovery of something important. I do not trust something within, and this prevents me from discovering who really supports us all. So what is this experience of facing poverty? It opens before me my total dependence on others for everything. Choosing poverty helps me to discover that dependence is actually a basic trust, the reliance upon my whole self in its interdependence with the universe. It is my mind in its separateness, and the anxiety arising from the separateness, that turns trust into negative insecurity of dependence.

By facing this anxiety and insecurity brought on by the idea of poverty, I am confronted with soul. For as we have seen in this short paper, the desire for creaturely comforts leads to insecurity and uncertainty because I cannot control my income, my ability to work, or even my faculties with which I work and earn. So I am forced to look within and listen when this fear of poverty arises. Thus I come upon soul work. In this way, the problem of money dissolves into the more basic question of "Who" is uncertain and "Who" meets uncertainty with work.

Who am I? I call myself a Jungian analyst and distinguish myself from others by virtue of my training and knowledge. Giving myself a special importance because of this, I create a division between myself and others in the same profession, and between myself and those who come as patients.

I also see a deeper division within me; by identifying myself with the work I do, I find myself dependent on the faculties which make that work possible. But the work I do occupies only a small part of my life. I work only when awake which occupies only part of the day. I am myself when in deep sleep, when dreaming, eating or relaxing. By identifying myself only with work, I narrow myself down to a few hours, and think as if all of me is that. I isolate myself from the total Self and the world. It is natural, therefore, for me to feel anxious and fearful upon discovering that my work can be lost at any time. Of course, I can try to make that isolated part appear whole by adding to it further parts of the same world, by joining groups, making money, learning more techniques, etc., to feel safe and secure. But this only makes me more identified with my work. Still, without work I lose my identity.

Having created hierarchies of values, distinctions, separations, and divisions within me and between me and the world, I attempt to meet the insecurity rooted in these divisions by receiving money. Instead of being the instrument of bridging, the 'medium of exchange,' money becomes the instrument of insecurity and separation. It leads me to forget the unique value of individual worth; it leads me to lose trust in who I really am; it leads me to lose trust in the world totality of which I am an organic part; it leads me to lose sight of soul work.

Reflections like these, which are themselves Soul Work, slowly bring me face to face with my No-thingness, and also at the same time with my utter dependence on wholeness within myself and with the universe. I want to be something, somebody, an unique 'I,' distinct from every other. But I cannot be anything alone. Perhaps the source of my insecurity and fear is that I do not really 'see' 'who' is so worried about insecurity . . . WHO AM I?

The Psyche, Wealth, and Poverty

By John Weir Perry

The invitation to me to speak on Soul and Money conceals a fine irony, given that I feel myself to be one of the most careless among my colleagues in money matters. I have committed all the sins of unconsciousness about money: after three decades I still tend to feel guilt over fees; I allow people to run up inordinate bills that sometimes go unpaid; billings go out late, and I drive my secretaries to distraction by relying on them to take care of such matters, and showing not a little impatience when complications arise. Whenever possible, I prefer not to think about money; I do so only at tax time, and my neck muscles tighten in protest. Although I realize that for many people money is the really real, for me it remains an abstraction, a set of numbers colored, I hope, black instead of red. At least I can speak for California, a state that first won fame for its *'aurum vulgaris,'* the 'common gold,' but now stands for something quite different: its notoriety made good during the last two decades by a beginning attempt to refine 'the true spiritual gold of the philosophers.'

With all this I felt that I would not have much to say on the topic until I began forcing myself to reflect on it. It soon became obvious that my 'sins' do not rise purely out of careless disregard, but rather out of attitudes that are ingrained, deeply. So my intention is to convey the various thoughts that appeared, and to capture their philosophic background. The fulcrum upon which they turn appears to be not money-making, but questions about the value of poverty.

As I looked back over the early signs of my inclination to avoid thinking about money, I recalled my school's motto emblazoned on its coat of arms and upon my mind: along with "Directness of Purpose" and "Self-Reliance," the one that best expressed the spirit of the school is "Simplicity of Life." I have never lost touch with that directive. I recalled also the crash of '29 and the ensuing depression. Most of us who were young then, and experienced firsthand the evanescence of riches, can never rely on money; other goals will always seem more enriching, and more dependable, than money-making.

Closer to home, though, was a choice my father made just on the verge of the crash. When his broker told him what was happening, advising him to get out while the getting was still possible, my father made an ethical decision not to do so, since that would be contributing even in small part to the general panic and the economy's downfall. It cost him; it cost all of us; yet I have always been glad for that example of a clearly moral action.

My father's courage in the face of panic and poverty reminded me of a couple of the best years I ever knew. During the second World War, I lived communally, with no money at all, as a member of the Friends Ambulance Unit in China. I particularly admired at that time the Maoist leaders in Shensi for their life-style of building and caring for their own homes, cut out of rugged loess, and Gandhi for his guiding the government of India from a simple tent in front of the government buildings.

Far in the background of my attitude to money lies the vivid awareness of widespread ancient teachings relating spiritual cultivation to voluntary poverty: that is, to develop spiritually it is important to divest oneself of too much concern with worldly welfare. Christianity, Taoism, Buddhism, and Islam share this view. We should not minimize the fact that spiritual cultivation has frequently been associated with voluntary poverty, because to do so leaves out of account considerations rooted in centuries of spiritual experience.

Seeking to learn more about the background of this association, and to fortify my paper with something solid, I went first to the *Britannica:* it had nothing whatsoever on the topic beyond socio-economic statistical studies. I turned next to Hasting's *Encyclopaedia of Religion and Ethics,* thinking it a sure bet because it had never failed me. Yet it did: there were only socio-economic researches; under monasticism, a passing mention of vows, along with chastity and obedience! In the works of Jung I could find nothing. Has it come to pass, I reflected, that our culture is so focused on the value of well-being that the value of poverty has been effaced? My initial research suggested so.

When I turned, however, to Evelyn Underhill's *Mysticism,* my quest found satisfaction: she explicates, lucidly and extensively, the motivation and rationale of voluntary poverty. For the mystics, it is entirely a question of what is most desired, and whether this results in separation or in a human-hearted connection with our fellow beings, a connection that culminates in an experience of the unity and mutual participation of all being in the One. Lusting after property, i.e., what you can possess as your own, fosters the divisiveness that nourished 'ego-motivations.' Property then defines one's identity—as that which is proper to oneself, much in the manner that the properties of a substance define its nature. The criterion of property provides a false basis for the differentiation of oneself and the world. The urgent desire to seek after God is considered incompatible with such desire for things of the world. Hence the Christian admonition, "You cannot serve both God and Mammon," or "It is easier for a camel to walk through the Eye of a needle than for a rich man to enter the Kingdom of Heaven." Yet to be poor in spirit, and therefore blessed, does not necessitate being poor in substance, but rather cleaving to a detachment as an inner state independent of outer conditions. The ultimate in this direction of thinking is such a renunciation of the world that one cannot live in it and needs a monastery to solve the dilemma.

When poverty is a true deprivation, it can, of course, become distracting and finally debilitating: one's attention remains fettered to the worries of survival. I am speaking here of a simplicity of life-style chosen freely and not imposed by external constraints and hardships. The great spirits who choose voluntary simplicity avoid the constraints of deprivation by living in a faith that assures them of their livelihood. From their faith a life-style evolves. We in our practices as therapists live in a faintly discernible version of such a faith. Without beating the bushes in the professional world to fill our practice, we nevertheless find that applicants for therapy present themselves at roughly the same pace at which they finish. One senses some sort of mysterious law of nature that seems to govern this flow that we cannot control.

We must ask at this point, facing the question honestly: is there anything wrong with the desire simply to make money handsomely in a practice? Many pitfalls lie on this road. Our current economy is demonstrating that as soon as the focus of caring is the paycheck and job security, merited or not, then the concern for quality of work declines. Analyst or auto mechanic: the same rule applies. We can easily, too, fall into the error of overvaluing the analytical profession, and permitting a drift toward inflated fees by consensual agreement. Our commodity for sale is our time, not our expertise. Our feeling, especially, cannot be bought, despite the American inclination to regard the gift of money as an expression of feeling. If an archetype of wealth reigns over our work, we encounter a dark underworld deity who, if I may play upon the word, might lead us to plutonic relationships. If we consider ourselves authorities paid for our knowledge, we court the danger of establishing inequality and non-mutuality with our clients who must labor to maintain us in this high station. The shadow of analysis, I sometimes think, is anything that separates us and our analysands.

A preference for simplicity in finances has its price. Prosperity allows one a great deal of free time to nourish the mind, and to maintain a tranquil pace in which reflectiveness and spiritual cultivation receive their due. Often I grumble at spending precious time typing letters, keeping accounts, and paying bills—even sometimes at building my house and grounds. Yet I am grateful for the grounding that these necessities have provided.

Early in my practice I decided that what I did not receive in fees I would make up by work with my hands, on house, furnishings and grounds. My children have learned to do the same. In essence, the governing thought in this way of being is "If you can't buy it, make it." Because of this I have not, insofar as I can recall, had to decline an applicant for therapy because of his inability to pay the fee requested. Nor have I had to limit my quarter-time participation in innovative programs because of the very low pay one receives (usually at an hourly rate which is one third of the standard fee in private practice). My three two-year experiences of this kind in innovative programs for therapy of schizophrenic young adults—the Agnew Project, Diabasis I and Diabasis II—have cost me more potential income than I like to calculate. No regrets, only some feeling of pinch—and a zestful race to stay a step ahead of the tax collectors.

In these projects I saw the divisiveness that money can create. The staff members who did all the heavy work of therapy and took care of the house were paid the least, while administration, the persona operations of our relationships with the mental health systems, received respectable salaries. I found myself in the awkward position of being paid at three times the hourly rate of the line staff, while at only one third of the professional fee rate of private practice. The inequality of the system caused many confrontations and objections; it took real effort to hold together in the face of these potential rifts.

Now, after making my pitch for simplicity of style, I must back up a little and remember that after all, my family and I live well by any socio-economic standard. Therefore my commitment is to a relative simplicity only, midway toward anything suggesting a voluntary poverty. This might be called a compromise, but that suggests weakness, an unconvinced half-heartedness. As I reflect about it, I find that it leads to a main point of my discussion. In our Jungian framework, we hold that when we live fully we take a position that holds us constantly in a state of sustaining paradoxes in the play of the opposites. According to this, in matters of finance we cannot choose either to renounce the world and its kind of well-being, nor allow our spiritual life to become sterile because of engulfment in worldly concerns. We must maintain both ends of the polarity in our lifestyles. We must hold to the midpoint.

Myth and Money

By Joel Covitz

I had two introductions to the role of money in psychoanalysis. The first came when I was studying at the Jung Institute, and a young analysand was negotiating a fee with me. I told him that my fee was twenty francs. Then we discussed the frequency of the visits, and we decided he would come three times a week. Then he asked me, "Would it be okay if I paid on the basis of three visits for fifty francs?"

My second introduction came from my dissertation on a Jewish dream book. The Talmud states that there was a dream interpreter, Bar Hedya, whose work depended on whether or not his fee were paid. Those dreamers who paid his fee received a positive interpretation; those who refused to pay received a negative interpretation.

Actually, money is an important element of an analyst's work with any patient. Everyone has a money complex, and the way each person relates to money can have a profound effect on other areas of his life. The ancient Greeks realized this when they correlated the absence of money with the disease process and its presence with the cure. Money is one of the "fundamental aspects of living reality." (Otto, 107) And in this paper, I want to address the psychological reality of money.

In our society, money is a necessity. Money *matters*. To the average employed or self-employed individual, money and its acquisition come to be extremely important. Western society is upwardly mobile. Many people in our civilization enter analysis partly because of their concern about their stations in life, often wanting to change classes and to move psychologically so that they suffer less from money problems. I want to restrict my comments here to individuals who begin with very little, who move on the path from nothing to something. I shall be less concerned with the use, investment, and spending of money than with its acquisition. I want to explore the development of what I call a "realistic attitude" toward the acquisition of money, because such acquisition must be one of the goals of an analysand trying to live in this society.

Now, money has traditionally had a rather negative 'press' in Western literature, reflecting a strong notion in our culture that affluence leads to decadence and the denial of the spirit. The Bible says that they that desire to be rich fall into a temptation and a snare and many foolish and hurtful lusts, such as drown men in destruction and perdition. For the love of money is the root of all kinds of evil: which some reaching after have been led astray from the faith: and have pierced themselves through with many sorrows. (I Tim. VI 9-10) The Puritan work ethic allows only for hard work and self-sacrifice—the notion that one should earn what one has by the sweat of one's brow, and that there should be no short-cuts, no easy way to wealth. Being in debt is frowned upon. But in our society, this is simply not a realistic attitude, as the case of Ralph will show.

In his youth, Ralph showed great promise. He wanted to be a doctor and tried to work his way through medical school while also supporting his family, but he found he couldn't do it. So he chose to drop out of medical school rather than to borrow money from the Government with a guaranteed loan. He thought that if he couldn't pay for school by himself, he shouldn't go. Ralph became a wreck; he never found a meaningful career. Years later, his wife left him. He wanted to marry again, but he had no means of earning a living. Then he entered analysis.

Now, this kind of refusal to get into debt is the wrong ethic for our culture. Ralph was really misled by the traditional work ethic. Debt belongs to a reliable person in our culture; it means one is creditable. To underestimate one's credit potential is to underestimate one's assets. Not to understand that is to be neurotic with regard to money, because it means one is living beneath one's potential. Part of the art of dealing with money is knowing how and when to go into debt, so that one can obtain the maximum potential from the money one borrows. As Benjamin Franklin said, "Money can beget money." (Franklin, 87) Many people—Thomas Jefferson was a prime example—live fruitful, creative lives without a lot of cash on hand. He was often in debt, but he lived to his fullest potential. Of course, this goes against the ethic which urges us to save rather than to borrow. But the person who will only save, who will not take risks with his money or security, who sees a concern with money as crass or 'dark' or 'shady,' will not succeed with money.

The traditional Puritan approach to money leaves behind many casualties—people with unhealthy approaches to money. Often the root of a family neurosis stems from some irresponsible treatment of one's assets. For instance, one analysand had a grandfather who was a millionaire. The millionaire's wife died when the millionaire was eighty and the old man remarried. He lived on for a few years and then died, and all of his money went to his new wife—a situation which disrupted the family. Also, it is often the children of millionaires who have to carry the shadow of their parents' wealth. The parents may consciously or unconsciously view their own acquisition of money as shady, so although they may pass on money, they also pass on ambivalent, paradoxical attitudes toward it. It is just possible that some of the destructive tendencies of children from wealthy families stem from this unconscious shadow-identification. They have the task of coming to terms with the acquisition of money, even if they themselves never had to acquire it.

In other ways the mishandling of money causes great trouble in the individual's adjustment. One patient of mine, John, neurasthenic and introverted, needed a push, and it never came. He lacked the energy even to ask for money. He knew his father had it, and he knew his father wouldn't give it to him. He was caught in the same situation as Hermes: a rich, unsupportive father. The difference was that Hermes reacted with tremendous initiative and was willing to make it on his own. But for children who are not gods, or are neurotic or depressed, nothing ever gets started. So John's father was a millionaire, and John was a do-nothing until the age of fifty, when his inheritance came. By then it was too late. The need for money helps you get out of the cave you are stuck in, with its low overhead; it gives you an incentive. The extreme case of lack of incentive might be seen in some Oriental and Christian sects, which advocate giving away all of one's possessions and money because the world will soon come to an end. (If this was Jesus' attitude, as has been argued, it was an error of predictive judgment.)

All of these problems I have just mentioned come from the lack of a realistic attitude about the need to acquire money in this society. There are a few important facts to keep in mind about money: it is a fact that money is never freely given away. You get nothing for nothing. And one should never depend on money being given. Money doesn't just come to you; you have to go after money, and this often requires that you be geographically mobile. And it is a fact that if you don't ask for money, you will never receive it. The Puritan fantasy is that wealth is not important. Other goals—honesty, hard work, generosity—have been given much better press. But one Puritan at least, Ben Franklin, talked about "procuring wealth, and thereby securing virtue; it being more difficult for a man in want to act always honestly, as . . . it is hard for an empty sack to stand upright." (Franklin, 92)

In fact, Franklin devoted a great deal of time and energy to the development of his theory of the "Way to Wealth," which involved remembering certain simple, but very realistic, and still applicable, laws about money. He said that "the use of money"—that is, the ability both to spend it and to make more money from it—"is all the advantage there is in having money." (80) "Time is money" and "credit is money." (87) Franklin knew that the primary way to get ahead is to invest one's money, or to lend it out at interest, since in that way even a small sum can be made to grow and grow. He also stressed the importance of saving: "a penny saved is a penny earned." If one plays by the rules and repays borrowed money on time, one can have an enormous amount of money at one's service: "He that is known to pay punctually," said Franklin, "may at any time, and on any occasion, raise all the money his friends can spare." (88) But he knew that one could not just sit back idly and expect to get rich; "the way to wealth," he said, "depends on [wasting] neither time nor money." (89) In *Poor Richard's Almanac*, where most of this wisdom was dispensed, he told his readers that "God helps them that help themselves." (95) What you have to do is take what the Fates bring you, and make the most of it.

What I would like to focus on now is just this art of affluence—recognizing the realistic need to have money in this society, and then marshaling all of one's forces, particularly the trickster who is in all of us, to reach that goal. The myth of the Greek god Hermes provides an archetype for this "trickster" psychology which allows for creative, flexible, daring approaches to the development of all possibilities in the individual, including the possibility of affluence.

As you know, Hermes was the son of Zeus and the nymph Maia. Soon after his birth, he felt restless in the dark cave, so he crept outside. He found a turtle going by. "What a great sign, what a help this is for me!" he said. "I won't ignore it." (Boer, 19) (Even at this tender age, he was open to the synchronicity of events.) So he tricked the turtle into coming into the cave with him. Then he took a knife and scooped the insides out of the shell and strung stalks of reed along it—and he had invented the lyre. The turtle had come along "at the rightful moment," (20) and Hermes had taken advantage of that moment. He was opportunistic.

Then Hermes found the sacred cattle of the gods and took fifty cows from the herd. He wanted to cover his tracks, so he devised a magical pair of sandals for himself so that his footprints could not be recognized. Then he reversed the tracks of the cows, "turning their front hooves backward and their back hooves frontward, while he himself walked backward." (23)

Now, while he was making his escape, an old man—a symbol for the old values—saw him walking away with the cows. Hermes said to him, "You didn't see what you just saw, okay? You didn't hear what you just heard. Keep quiet and you won't get hurt." (24) And Hermes made it safely back, slaughtered two of the cows, and sacrificed them properly. Then he threw his magical sandals away—tricksters have to pay close attention to details like that—and went back to the cave. His mother knew he had been up to no good.

Hermes told her not to worry, however, since he would provide for her:

> Nay, we do not wish to sit amongst the gods without gifts or prayers, as is thy plan! Surely it is better to sport for all eternity amongst the immortals, in inexhaustible wealth, rather than to cower here in this gloomy cave! I mean to win the same sacred reverence as is paid to Apollo! Unless my father grants me this, I shall pluck up the courage—and I can do it!—to become a prince of thieves. (Kerenyi, 165)

With the goal of inexhaustible, as opposed to expendable, wealth to encourage him, Hermes was determined to make his fortune, doing whatever it took to gain the same stature—and wealth—as his more famous brother, Apollo.

Meanwhile, Apollo had obviously noticed the significant decrease in the size of his herd of cattle. He tracked Hermes down and demanded the return of the cows. Hermes pretended complete innocence: he didn't have any information, he said, about the theft. It was ridiculous to suppose that a tiny baby could steal fifty cows. Apollo laughed at this clever story and called Hermes a trickster, and insisted that Hermes lead the way to the cows. Hermes complained that he had been falsely accused. So they went to see their father, Zeus, who told each to plead his case. Apollo told his story, and then Hermes spoke in his own defense: "Father Zeus, I'm going to tell you the truth. I'm a frank person, and I don't know how to lie," he said. "I didn't take his cattle home, though I do want to be rich." (Boer, 45) At this, Zeus burst out laughing, ordered the brothers to reconcile their differences, and told Hermes to show Apollo where the cows were hidden. Apollo was still angry, so Hermes decided to calm him by playing the lyre. And he played so beautifully that Apollo was charmed, and said that Hermes' music was *worth* fifty head of cattle. He promised Hermes immortal glory among the gods if only he would teach him this art. Always on the alert for a fair exchange, Hermes agreed, provided he could have the cattle. So Apollo got the lyre, and Hermes got glory and the use of the cattle. Then Apollo "presented Hermes with a further gift, a golden three-leaved staff, which bestows wealth." (Kerenyi, 170) From then on, Hermes was in charge of exchanges and commerce among men and was glorified among the gods.

The first thing to note about the story of Hermes is that he knew he could not stay in his gloomy cave. He needed to get out, into a house with a view. He did not wait for his father's inheritance; rather, he took his fate into his own hands and extraverted his affluent fantasy. When faced with the trap of poverty, he realized his dream of wealth while remaining in the company of the gods. "I will try whatever plan is best, and so feed myself and you continuously!" he said to his mother. (Hesiod) He developed a positive view, a system for becoming affluent, starting with nothing but his wits and his envy.

Hermes' style is unique. There is something very appropriate about his inappropriateness. Sometimes, going backward is going forward. His methods were trickster methods—clever theft rather than barefaced robbery, story-telling, the ability to get Zeus and Apollo to laugh instead of to curse. Hermes was a master at getting himself out of a tight spot by telling a story. The world responds to a story whether it's true or not. If you want a loan and you tell the banker the wrong story, he can't give you the loan; so if you are in touch with the trickster in your psyche, you tell the banker the right story. To tell the truth in some situations is a sign of masochism. You have to be daring and take risks to get anywhere. Hermes knew that Apollo and Zeus didn't believe his tales of innocence, but it is the story itself that counts: he made them laugh at it. The art of convincing people is an important part of the art of affluence.

At first the question arises: isn't Hermes just a common criminal? The trickster who steals cattle and then lies about it may not seem particularly praiseworthy. But there are several differences between the trickster-figure and the criminal. For one, the criminal, separated from and angry at his culture, cannot identify with the collective whole. But the Hermetic person knows the power structure and works within his culture. He looks for loopholes, for back roads, but he is not a criminal; he is merely trying to be more clever than the mainstream. The sociopath, for example, evades paying taxes; the Hermetic man, instead, finds tax shelters. Part of the key to Hermes' success is that he knew the rules within which he had to work. He knew how, when, and what to sacrifice; he stole the cattle, but hungry as he was he did not ruin the sacrifice by eating any of the meat. In the words of Rafael Lopez-Pedraza, "the classic Jungian concept [of sacrifice] is based on what is sacrificed as already being worn out, which gives it a Hermetic touch." (37)

Even though Hermes is a thief, he has a Robin Hood style—attempting to restore society's proper equilibrium. "Though much of this must seem questionable from a moral point of view," says Walter Otto, "nevertheless it is a configuration which belongs to the fundamental aspects of living reality." (107) We must assume that the individual who starts with nothing has to be a bit unethical. The trickster is not only conscious of the formal laws of society; he is also aware of custom and culture—taking into account, for example, the American ethical principle "thou shalt not get caught." The Hermetic man in Russia is the Communist who is still able to get caviar.

In setting his goal as "inexhaustible wealth," Hermes was confident and resourceful; he knew he could do it, although he didn't at first know how. He created from what was at hand, thus displaying the flexibility which is central to the Hermetic approach. A master of the art of collage, of combination, he was open to accidental discoveries, and in this way he participated in his own fate.

Hermes was traditionally the god of exchanges of goods and money between men; he was the god of boundaries, where neighboring tribes met to exchange and facilitate economic growth. Hermes was considered "a source of material blessings" for men. (Brown, 22) His staff brings wealth, and he promotes exchanges which benefit both parties, just as his exchange with Apollo benefited both of them. In ancient Greece, "mutual permission to steal" (Brown, 42) was recognized as a kind of trade, but it actually was a kind of gift exchange.

Gift exchanges are important. When an unfair exchange takes place, the delicate balance of money and power is disrupted. John, about whom I told you before, was always getting the wrong gifts; he never really got what he needed. He got ripped off in the exchange with his parents. Understanding gift-giving is similar to knowing how to deal with money, and John's father couldn't handle either one. The sentimental view, of course, is that one gives out of selflessness and love. But really, gift-giving is often setting up the possibility for an exchange at no real cost to either party. The gift is an exchange of power. From the Hermetic point of view, giving is receiving. Gift-giving can be seen, then, as an investment.

The point is not accumulating money just for its own sake, but rather having a Hermetic style, which will help constellate positive experiences. The Hermetic person will find that he has more energy to accomplish things; that he is in a position of power and can work toward achieving his own potential while also having a possible role in influencing the destiny of his culture. Money is the means to an end.

*

So the next question is, how can we apply the Hermetic principles to analytical work? How can we encourage analysands to develop the trickster in their psyches? The Hermetic approach promotes self-help, resourcefulness, independence, and flexibility. To encourage the acquisition of subtle, daring techniques in a patient is not unethical. In addition to promoting the trickster in a patient, the analyst must become a trickster figure himself. Norman O. Brown says, "In the modern view . . . we regard cheating as the antithesis of good workmanship. Hence modern scholars have felt obliged to brand the cult of Hermes the 'tricky' as immoral . . . but his function is to promote human welfare," (23) just as the analyst must promote his patients' welfare.

The Greeks used to call any lucky find that a traveler chanced upon a "gift of Hermes." (Brown, 41) The art of seeing possibilities in chance occurrences, in synchronicities, is of course at the heart of Jungian thought. When my patient, John, was eight years old, he found a twenty-dollar bill in the Kennedy Airport parking lot, and he rejoiced in his "lucky find." But his grandfather, who was not engaged with the trickster side of himself, admonishingly instructed John to return the money to the place he had found it, saying, "You may not know whose it is, but you know it isn't yours."

The trickster approach also encourages independence on the part of the patient. Having broken free of his father, Hermes was able to provide for himself and thus take his rightful place on Olympus with the family gods. Hermes said, "If my father will not provide, then I can, and I am able." The lack of money is often correlated with the lack of flexibility in life; in addition to cutting down on geographical mobility, it can prove to be a kind of psychic paralysis—a paralysis both of psychic movement internally and life movement externally. The Hermetic approach allows a person to feel free to follow his soul, his destiny; it frees up his psychic energy in order to enable him to actualize his soul.

It is known that the positive role of envy in the psyche is to show the individual what potentially can be his. Hermes' envy of Apollo's wealth and stature motivated him to fulfill his own potential. Envy often serves such a motivating force within the family. My son once asked my wife, "If I join the Boston Symphony, will I earn as much as Daddy?" At a young age, he was already using a Hermetic sense of competition as a motivation.

I had one analysand, Debra, who together with her husband mastered the non-Hermetic art of mere survival. They were what I call the lowest common denominator type—low rent, Salvation Army clothes, but money in the bank. They were content with low overhead—with the cave. Their system had a built-in breakdown point, however, which occurred when their daughter entered drama school, confronting them with the need to earn more money to pay the yearly $7,500 for her tuition and board. As could be expected, Debra and her husband, with their non-Hermetic style, constellated their daughter's adoption of a Hermetic one. While Debra had been saving her limited funds in the bank, their daughter was developing her acting career, working as a television actress all through high school and earning much of the money for her schooling herself.

How can you generate the trickster in a patient? As a Jungian analyst, you can recognize the trickster when it makes an appearance in the material of the unconscious, and make sure to point it out to the analysand. Note how the trickster appears in dreams and fantasies, and try to integrate it as a basic part of the patient's personality. The analyst should observe when the lack of connection with the trickster gets in the way of the progress of a patient who is "serious and inflexible." He or she should also observe how the trickster is projected into the relationship with the analyst and offer this interpretation to the analysand.

The acquisition of money and its relationship to the soul are reflected in the artist, writer, actor, poet, musician, and even the analyst, who most people say is more of an 'artist' than practitioner. Jung represented this point of view when he said that he would be willing to change all of his theories for the benefit of any one patient.

What about the artist who cannot support himself? The artist who has not solved his money-maintenance dilemma may be a genius, but he is also ill in a money-archetypal sense. If you find that you can't support yourself as an artist, perhaps you should consider giving up being an artist. The problem of the artist, if he sees his money coming from the practice of his art, is to figure out *how* to earn money from art. Many neurotic artists are non-flexible . . . "I can only work on this size canvas, in this medium . . . . " This kind of thinking is often rigid and limiting, whereas true artists are usually flexible. Many of the great masters of painting throughout history have worked on commission. Aside from the very few artists who are ahead of their times, the unsuccessful, neurotic artist is often either not talented enough or too inflexible. Jung warns against the "hobby artists" who try to make professions of their hobbies.

One variable to examine in the actor, musician, poet, and artist is the degree of *necessity.* How connected is the soul to the particular activity or craft? What is the soul's investment in this endeavor, and how deeply rooted is the commitment? Often when the talent is lacking, the soul and libido are elsewhere, which will be reflected in the material of the unconscious. It may sound crude to think of art in terms of its earning power, but the artist must come to terms with financial reality. To work on 'inner vision' without outer verification in the form of financial acknowledgment is reserved for the very few, or very rich.

Is the person who uses Hermetic tricks to make a little money, to get a start in the world, getting something for nothing? No. He is getting something for cleverness. The trickster will go out in search of affluence. The "welfare mentality" could be an exercise in self-deception; the fantasy of the welfare recipient is that he is getting something for nothing. But is having to sacrifice one's self-esteem nothing? The recipient who thinks he is getting a good deal is being tricked by his own trick. Nothing comes from nothing. I am reminded of the story in Studs Terkel's book *Working,* where the hooker tells of her initial delight in making fifty dollars in twenty minutes, and coming out of it feeling unchanged. It was only years later, demoted in status from call girl to streetwalker and heroin addict, that she realized the price she had paid for that money. She was tricked by her own trick. One can also be tricked by the trick of marrying a rich spouse, since that decreases one's incentive to achieve one's potential. In Jung's words, it may also decrease one's sense of viability. An analyst does not want his patients to be tricked by their own tricks; if he can encourage them to be resourceful, flexible and daring, so much the better.

In 1911, Jung and Freud carried on the following dialogue on what Jung called the problem of the "failure of the rich marriage." Freud wrote to Jung,

> Give your charming, clever, and ambitious wife the pleasure of saving you from losing yourself in the business of money-making. My wife often says she would be only too proud if she were able to do the same for me . . . . Your taste for money-making already worried me in connection with your American dealings. On the whole, it will prove to be good business if you forego ordinary pursuits. Then, I am sure, extraordinary rewards will come your way.

Jung replied,

> It's not all that bad with my money-making . . . . I need a large practice in order to gain experience, for I do not imagine that I know too much. Also, I have had to demonstrate to myself that I am able to make money in order to rid myself of the thought that I am non-viable. These are all frightful stupidities which can only be overcome by acting them out. (436-437)

Women today may be expressing Jung's point of view when they equate viability with earning money. In former times, women may have found affirmation and acknowledgment from non-monetary sources; however, these seem to be lacking today.

What does the Hermetic point of view mean to the analyst himself? Hermes, who was the god of craftsmen, of men who made money from their labor and, in some myths, of healers, is a significant archetypal figure for analysts. Lopez-Pedraza says that ''in spite of Hermes' marginal, crooked, trickster, thief and cheater aspects, paradoxically, we can give full recognition to him in his role as protector of psychotherapy,'' since ''psychological thieving''—which any analyst frequently indulges—is the ''natural and basic activity of Hermes in the psyche.'' (31) Healers throughout history have been highly paid. Pliny once complained that healers made ''enormous amounts of money.'' (Majno, 348) As healers, we are lucky to have the god of commerce on our side.

The fluctuation of the therapist's financial state, of course, is a subject of great concern to most of us. An old maxim says that a patient must fulfill two obligations to his analyst: he must punctually attend his agreed-upon sessions, and he must consistently pay his bill. We all know what happens to our affectionate and humanitarian feelings when the patient refuses to pay his bill. It is even more intolerable than when he stands you up for his session, and 'accidentally' represses his capacity to use the telephone to notify you. Recall the story I related at the beginning of this paper about the Talmudic dream interpreter who modified his interpretation according to the dreamer's payment. A fourteenth-century commentary on this passage interpreted it to mean that when the dreamer failed to pay, the dream interpreter acted toward the dreamer as an ''enemy in revenge.''

Even Freud, the first to practice our Hermetic craft, worried and wrote a great deal about the relationship of money and therapy. His early letters to Wilhelm Fliess contain many references to the important role money played in his thoughts about his practice. In 1095, he noted that he was in a position to "pick and choose and begin to dictate my fees," (136) and he talked of "earning the recompense that I need for my well-being." (173) "It suits me best to have a lot of work," he wrote in 1897. "I earned 700 florins last week, for instance, and you do not get that for nothing." (192) But he added, "It must be very difficult to get rich." (192) He kept on "worrying and saving," (218) as he put it.

Later, things took a turn for the worse; the summer season was nearly always painfully slow for him, and this depressed him a good deal. He told Fliess, "We are like to *schnorrers* [beggars]" (211) and went on to complain that he was impoverished, without enough work, having to take on new patients constantly—and even to take on some without a fee, simply to keep from getting too bored. He was worried that his financial troubles would begin to interfere with his self-analysis, and he felt that, since he was so tired and depressed, his patients were not getting their money's worth. "It is a pity," he wrote, "one cannot live on dream-interpretation." (218) (Which is what Jungian analysts might be said to do.) His financial worries left him in a "mental and material depression," (327) and he noted that "a bad mental state is no more productive than economizing is." (322) His "one weak point, my fear of poverty," (318) was contrasted with his dreams of wealth: "The hope of eternal fame was so beautiful, and so was that of certain wealth, complete independence, travel, and removing the children from the sphere of the worries which spoiled my own youth." (217-18) "Today," he wrote, "after twelve hours' work and earning 100 florins, I am again at the end of my strength .... Just as art only thrives in

the midst of prosperity, so do aspirations only thrive with leisure.''
(275)

Thus Freud understood that the analyst could only do his best
work when freed from his own neurotic constraints, one of which
could be the lack of money. You can only do good work when you
are not sick yourself. Freud's equation of the lack of money with a
''mental and material depression'' is in the Greek tradition of seeing poverty as part of the disease process. This theme is fully
elaborated in C.A. Meier's book, *Ancient Incubation and Modern
Psychotherapy.*

The patient-analyst relationship is an exchange; the analyst carries
the problems of the patient for a fee. The analysand gets what he
pays for. Thomas Jefferson expressed this notion: Never buy what
you do not want because it is cheap; it will be dear to you. I have at
home an ad for paint which states: ''Don't blame the painter. If the
painter has to use cheap materials to meet your price ideas, you've
no kick coming if the job doesn't last. Pay a fair price for good
honest varnish, enamel and paint.'' I often feel that the same truth
can apply to an analyst.

This leads to a last and controversial question: whether or not
analysts should charge for interviews that patients miss. The rule
that you charge whether or not the patient shows up is in the Hermetic tradition: the analyst is thus providing for himself, making
sure that he can support himself, and not resenting his patients.
Freud belonged to this Hermetic tradition, even though he sometimes took on patients who could not pay; he knew that he needed
the stability of an income for his family and himself in order to be
able to do good work. The idea is that the patient is not receiving
help only during the session; the analyst has invested his time and
energy in the whole process of analysis, and deserves to be paid for

it. Frieda Fromm-Reichmann seems to agree with this point of view when she says,

> Psychiatric services . . . are priceless if successful or worthless if they fail. It is through these attempts, nevertheless, that the therapist makes his living, so that the settlement of his fees has to be determined by the market value of psychiatric services at a given time and in a given area . . . . If [a] patient repeatedly misses interviews for invalid reasons, warning should be given, and thereafter charges should be made. (67)

But on the next page of the same book, she apparently contradicts herself: "it is not the psychiatrist's privilege to be exempt from the generally accepted custom of our culture in which one is not paid for services not rendered." (68) I suggest that the Hermetic approach is a sound one to the resolution of this tricky problem, but many analysts, I realize, might not feel comfortable with it.

Jung, too, was a trickster sort of fellow; he said once that he went into the practice of psychoanalysis because he thought he could earn more money at it than he could from his first love, archaeology. "I hadn't the money," he said, "to be an archaeologist . . . . I never thought I had any chance to get any further, because we had no money at all . . . . [But] a doctor can develop . . . he can choose his scientific interests." (McGuire, 428) However, Jung didn't have to earn a living from his practice, and as a result, some people claimed he often undercharged his patients. This infuriated some of his fellow analysts because it inadvertently undervalued analysis, and it embarrassed them about their own fees. Jung seemed to them to be insensitive to the acquisition of money from an analytic practice. He may not have fully realized that, most often, analysts were healers who were selling their expertise in order to provide for themselves. His Hermeticism seemed not to extend to the realm of money. I wonder why. Was it that he retained an old idea of medicine as Christian charity? Or was it perhaps that he felt guilty about the source of his own money?

I'd like to close with two quick stories. One is an ancient Jewish tale from the thirteenth century, which illustrates the maxim "you get what you pay for." One day a Gentile was sitting, depressed. His friend said to him, "Why is your face so downtrodden?" and he answered, "I saw in a dream that I was riding on a red horse and the horse was near an impure platform." His friend said to him, "that means that you will quickly die in your bed." And then the dream interpreter said to him, "If you give me something to drink, I will purchase the dream from you." He replied, "On this condition I will give it to you—that my dream will be sold to you." And he gave the dream interpreter something to drink, and the dream interpreter died the second day after that.

And finally, C.A. Meier tells us that in ancient Greece, "after the cure, the former patient was expected to pay certain fees and make thank offerings. We have on record instances in which the god administered a sharp lesson to tardy debtors . . . by promptly ordaining a relapse." (316)

Boer, Charles, trans., *The Homeric Hymns,* 2nd ed., revised, Spring Publications, Inc., Irving, Texas, 1979.

Brown, Norman O., *Hermes the Thief: The Evolution of a Myth,* Vintage Books, Random House, New York, New York, 1947.

Franklin, Benjamin, *Works,* Volume 2.

Freud, Sigmund, *The Origins of Psychoanalysis: Letters to Wilhelm Fliess, Drafts and Notes, 1887-1902,* Basic Books, Inc., New York, New York, 1954.

Fromm-Reichmann, Frieda, *Principles of Intensive Psychotherapy,* University of Chicago Press, Chicago, Illinois, 1950.

Hesiod, trans. Hugh G. Evelyn-White, *The Homeric Hymns and Homerica,* Loeb Classical Library, Harvard University Press, Cambridge, Massachusetts, 1914.

Kerenyi, C., *The Gods of the Greeks,* Thames and Hudson, London, 1951.

Lopez-Pedraza, Rafael, *Hermes and His Children,* Spring Publications, Zurich, 1977.

Majno, Guido, *The Healing Hand: Man and Wound In The Ancient World,* Harvard University Press, Cambridge, Massachusetts, 1975.

McGuire, William, and R.F.C. Hull, eds., *C.G. Jung Speaking,* Princeton University Press, Princeton, New Jersey, 1977.

Meier, C.A., *Ancient Incubation and Modern Psychotherapy.*

Otto, Walter, trans. Moses Hadas, *The Homeric Gods,* Thames and Hudson, London, 1951.

Terkel, Studs, *Working.*

Von Grunebaum, G.E., and Roger Caillois, eds., *The Dream and Human Societies,* University of California Press, Berkeley, 1966.

Projections: Soul and Money

By Adolf Guggenbühl-Craig

I have yet to meet the person who is indifferent to money. *Soul and Money* is the title of this book. Now 'soul' is a difficult term to use. Some psychologists avoid it, trying to create a psychology without soul. Others replace the religious-sounding 'soul' with the more neutral 'psyche.' I am all for employing the word 'soul,' yet, when used too often, it sounds pompous or sentimental. There is no way out: if you don't use the word ''soul'' you avoid the basic issue of psychology; use it too often and it becomes embarrassing.

Soul is and remains a mystery. What is it? Where is it? How is it? We cannot catch it, we cannot locate it; soul is everywhere and nowhere. Because of its elusiveness, we have to experience and recognize soul mainly through projection. Projecting the soul enables us to deal with it.

Throughout history soul has been projected onto many things, human and non-human. Sexuality—as an act and the fantasies about it—is a great projection carrier for soul. The development and individuation of soul are lived in and symbolized by sexuality.

Although I said that soul is elusive, let me assign the soul a few characteristics, acknowledging that these characteristics are arbitrary and subjective. First: secrecy. Wherever soul appears, there is secrecy, a secrecy that is expressed through many symbols. Initiation rituals designed to connect to soul are shrouded in secrecy. The soul is often depicted as a hidden treasure in the woods, guarded by dragons in caves, etc. Second: fascination. Being concerned with one's soul is not just a pastime; it is an obsession, a passion. Finding one's soul is the greatest aim in life; losing it the greatest calamity. Third: strength and energy. The loss of soul results in weakness, while being in touch with soul produces boundless energy.

After this arbitrary enumeration of some qualities of the soul, consider sexuality, a main projection carrier of soul.

Even today most people keep sexual matters secret. Few would ever make love in public. Although we now talk more about our sexual lives, this often means only that we lie more about it. Hardly anybody tells the 'truth' about his sexual life. Yet, from the so-called natural point of view, there is no need for secrecy in sexuality. As a tool of relationship or pure pleasure, sexuality could be lived out openly, publicly. Why not tell everyone about it? The secrecy connected with sexuality appears to be unnatural and irrational. It comes from the soul projection on sexuality.

To mention that many experience sexuality in an obsessive compulsive way is almost redundant. At times in their lives almost everyone fails to contain sexuality, and is driven to live it out, or is at least obsessed by sexual fantasies. The third characteristic of soul, strength and energy, so closely connects to soul that one of the greatest psychologists ever, Sigmund Freud, equated sexuality with psychic energy. He confused the projection carrier of soul with the thing itself.

Now my thesis: *money, also, is a main projection carrier for soul.* As with sexuality, so are secrecy, obsession, and energy qualities of money.

While the secrecy that cloaks money matters varies with each individual and culture, most people in the Western world conceal money matters one way or another. Often, we just lie. Like all tales about sexuality, stories about money fall short of the truth. The stories are a personal mythology. And as with sexuality, no objective reason offers itself as an explanation for such secrecy. What objective reason is there to hide our net worth, our yearly income from friends and enemies, and even our children?

Money also fascinates us, often in peculiar ways. We may imagine that the rich are different, and solely because they have more money. We then feel slightly inferior in the presence of rich people; many analysts have difficulty treating them. I know a colleague—his practice has a special parking space for clients—who starts sweating with anxiety each time he notices that a new patient drives a very expensive car!

Some people are over-thrifty and cannot part with their money despite a comfortable income and no financial worries. Interesting is a little experience which a wealthy friend of mine told me. He saw how a lady received a lot of small coins as change in a shop, making her purse feel rather heavy. When she left the shop, she threw the coins—worth perhaps two dollars—into the gutter because they were simply too heavy to carry. Deeply shocked, my friend *had* to pick up the coins. Throwing coins into the gutter just *is not done;* it would be the same as flushing sacramental wine down the toilet. This 'numinous' half-religious quality of money can be understood only as a projection. Money itself is a technical means of exchange, possessing no second nature, nothing 'numinous.'

That we connect money with the life-force is obvious. Old people who deny themselves every luxury, and complain bitterly about the price of heating, electricity, food, etc. sometimes leave large fortunes behind when they die. The awareness that life or energy is running out leads them to compensate by piling up money, that is, energy.

Although economists often assume the profit motive to be a fundamental drive animating human behavior, we psychologists know that few people, especially the successful ones, really work for money. For instance, I know a very successful paint manufacturer who believes that he works to make lots of money. And yet when you talk to him longer than ten minutes, you see that what actually fascinates him is paint, the different colors and their effect on people.'

If you live in Zurich, it's almost impossible not to notice that strength and power are projected on money. Foreigners talk of the 'gnomes of Zurich.' They imagine Zurich bankers as all-powerful manipulators who control the economic ups and downs of the whole world. There was even an English minister who blamed the Swiss gnomes for the weakness of the pound! Yet these Zurich bankers are as helpless in trying to understand or manipulate the money market as we analysts sometimes are towards a highly psychotic patient.

Money is a tremendous projection carrier. Because money is so faceless, so neutral, we tend to project on it more easily. But because it is so important, we have great difficulty knowing where projections start and where money itself begins. Nearly everything can be projected on money: power, security, sexuality and, in some bizarre way, even reality. Some people think that money is *the reality,* the *real thing.*

*

We take transference and counter-transference in analysis very seriously, rightly so. The patient reveals himself by what he projects on the analyst and vice-versa. In these mutual projections soul appears. The Freudians say—or said—that the therapist should be a white screen on which the patient can project his whole psyche. However, we analysts are not white screens! The patient not only projects on us; what he sees and experiences with us is influenced by what we are.

Money, however, *is a white screen*. We all project onto money those particular qualities characteristic of our personal psyches. One question I want to ask is: Why do we not look at this screen more often? Only lately have I realized that a proper analysis must include an extensive contemplation of the patient's and analyst's projections onto money. I think that we are a little wary of this topic because it touches us as analysts too deeply. Not only the patient, but we too project our specific soul on faceless money.

As with all soul things, so much lying goes on between patient and analyst concerning money. Some patients complain of the hardship worked on them by the fee, yet are actually well off, while others pay so cheerfully that the analyst is later surprised to learn that the fee represents a great sacrifice. Despite our expectation that the patient be honest in everything—including money matters—we analysts often refuse to answer point-blank questions about our income, or we lie.

Of money in relationships: the give-and-take of money is, projectively, experienced repeatedly as the loss or gain of soul. Money often causes trouble between parents and their offspring. A thirty-year-old man spent his vacation regularly with wife and children at his parents' home, accepting his parents' hospitality without qualms. But when his father offered financial help so that the son could buy a house he wanted, the son refused. As a result he could not buy the house. The son was afraid of losing his independence, or, really, 'losing his soul' by taking money. Financial independence often means psychological independence. Money relationship is ex-

87

perienced as soul relationship.

So much can be seen in our connection to money: our kind of greed and generosity, the way we love and hate, what we fear and what we hope to achieve in life. Psycho-pathologists know that psychotic depression often has a link to money. A very rich man who becomes depressively psychotic thinks he will soon starve to death because his money will not last. This is, of course, an extreme. More interesting and more important in our daily practices are the subtle projections we all have on money.

What about: "Money is the root of all evil"?

For so many people, money is evil, nasty, destructive. Rich people are bad. Money corrupts. You all know the saying in the New Testament: "It is easier for a camel to pass through the eye of a needle than for a rich man to enter the kingdom of Heaven." Christianity has always deemed money as something essentially evil.

The same is true about sexuality. Christianity has every reason to consider money and sexuality as evil because *sexuality and money are the two great projection carriers for soul.* As I said: most of us project our own soul on these two things, or at least one of them. In this way sexuality and money compete with religion. Christianity asks that you project your soul and its development, its individuation, on Jesus Christ. Worldly projections of our soul distract us from the Christian aim of salvation of our soul through Jesus Christ. To put it bluntly: the great competitors for the salvation of our soul through Jesus Christ are sexuality and money. Insofar as sexuality and money detract from salvation through Jesus Christ, they are evil.

The aim of analysis—as a cure or as a way of individuation, as soul-finding—cannot be to withdraw all our projections, but to become aware of them, and to live them out intensively. Our very lives—our individuation—consist in projecting our souls on sexuality, on money, on our partner, our children, our jobs, etc., and we individualize through these. The aim of analysis is not to hinder someone from falling in love, but to love more passionately with occasional reflection. The aim is to live our projections, hold on to them, while seeing that they are projections, that most of our deeds are only symbolic rituals.

Should we, when approaching the projections on money, try to eliminate them, withdraw them, or should we even foster them?

The answer is obvious: we should certainly not eliminate and destroy the soul projections we and our patients have on money. We should even foster them if the patient is inclined to do so. Projections of soul on money have advantages over other projections. What we experience through money, what we project on money, is so clearly a projection, a fact well-known, and deeply engraved on the collective psyche. Projections of soul on money are so easy to recognize—much easier than projections of soul on relationships or art. In some ways it is desirable that we project our soul on money.

In a somewhat twisted variation of the biblical saying about the rich man, I would say that a man or woman who can project his soul on money has as good a chance as anyone of going to heaven.

NOTES

NOTES

NOTES

NOTES